TENNESSEE WONDERS

A Pictorial Guide to the Parks

Text by

MIKE CARLTON

Photographs by

JOHN NETHERTON

Foreword by
Senator Howard H. Baker

RUTLEDGE HILL PRESS

NASHVILLE, TENNESSEE

The state park descriptions on pages 122–28 are used by permission of the Division of State Parks
of the Tennessee Department of Environment and Conservation.

**Published in Nashville, Tennessee,
by Rutledge Hill Press,
211 Seventh Avenue North, Nashville, Tennessee 37219.**

Typography by Gary Gore

Library of Congress Cataloging-in-Publication Data

Carlton, Mike, 1959–
    Tennessee wonders : a pictorial guide to the parks / text by Mike Carlton ;
photographs by John Netherton ; foreword by Howard H. Baker
      p.   cm.
    ISBN 1-55853-289-7
    1. Parks—Tennessee—Pictorial works. 2. Natural areas—Tennessee—
Pictorial works. 3. Tennessee—Pictorial works. 4. Parks—Tennessee.
5. Natural areas—Tennessee. 6. Tennessee—Description and travel.
I. Netherton, John. II. Title.
F437.C37 1994
917.6804´53—dc20   94-5228
                                                      CIP

Printed in Mexico

1 2 3 4 5 6 7 8 9 — 99 98 97 96 95 94

Contents

Foreword

When I announced that I was retiring from the U.S. Senate and would not stand for reelection in 1984, members of the press descended on me in hordes. Each proclaimed that incumbent majority leaders simply did not behave like this. I explained my reasoning, and everyone seemed to understand at least partially why I was leaving public service. One particularly insistent reporter for the *Washington Post*, however, was incredulous that I planned on returning to my home in Tennessee. "You have risen to the very height of power in Washington and have been here for almost twenty years, how can you possibly return to a place like Tennessee?" he asked. I replied, "Because it is the absolute center of the universe!"

I still feel that way, and if you spend a little time with *Tennessee Wonders* by John Netherton and Mike Carlton, you will begin to realize why. Tennessee is more like three states than one. East Tennessee, where I live, is a land of mountains, valleys, and rugged people who cherish their independence. Our music—filled with the sounds of fiddles, dulcimers, and dancers clogging—comes straight from our Irish and Scottish ancestors. Middle Tennessee is a land of rolling hills, hollows, Tennessee Walking Horses, and country music with a Nashville sound. West Tennessee is different still. A broad, flat land where cotton is king, it draws its life from the Mississippi River. The music of West Tennessee is Memphis blues, New Orleans jazz, and rock 'n' roll.

The differences among the three Grand Divisions of Tennessee are reflected in their parks. The Great Smoky Mountain National Park may be the best-known park in East Tennessee, but I am partial to Big South Fork, which is in my back yard. Both offer mountains to climb, rugged beauty, and an abundance of wild flowers. Radnor Lake in Nashville reflects the charm of Middle Tennessee. I am always struck that this bit of wilderness lies within our state's capital city. West Tennessee's orientation to the Mississippi is best felt at Meeman-Shelby State Park, which overlooks the mighty river.

Mike Carlton and John Netherton have given Tennesseans and visitors a wonderful gift in providing this guide to the state's parks. The seventeen parks on which they focus are representative of all the parks in the state.

Mike speaks with the voice of a park tour guide. You can almost hear him warn about a loose rock here or a slippery area over there. He has worked in Tennessee's parks for almost fourteen years and knows them as if he had laid out the design for each himself.

Few people have the gift John does for capturing nature on film. He and I have photographed the parks of Tennessee together for several years, and we collaborated on *Big South Fork Country*, a book of photographs he and I took. John's photographs have a rich composition and color. If you look carefully, you may see the water flow, the trees sway, and the animals blink.

We Tennesseans can be proud of our parks. The Tennessee park system is one of the best in the United States. I hope you enjoy this guide, but be sure also to enjoy the parks themselves. They were made for you.

Howard H. Baker

Introduction

From the broad Mississippi River floodplain in the west to the Great Smoky Mountains in the east, Tennessee contains some of America's most picturesque parks and natural areas. East and Middle Tennessee offer striking geological features and scenic overlooks where the forces of nature forged mountains, carved gorges, and created waterfalls. Wildlife is plentiful in the parks of West Tennessee because it thrives on the region's many rivers and lakes. This is one of the few remaining areas in the United States where it is not unusual to see the national symbol—the Bald Eagle—soar against a clear, blue sky.

Many of the parks of Tennessee were born as projects during the New Deal under the Works Progress Administration and the Civilian Conservation Corps. Today, the Tennessee State Park System oversees more than fifty parks and is one of the most diverse and best-developed systems in the country. This widespread system was designed so that every Tennessean could be within an hour's drive of one of the parks. The system offers many varieties of parks, including day-use, resort and rustic parks, and cultural, archaeological, and natural areas. Within the state park system, resort facilities include eight golf courses, seven resort hotels and inns, and fourteen restaurants. No fewer than seventeen parks have rustic and modern cabins, and camping is offered in at least forty parks. Almost every park provides hiking and nature trails. Because of the numerous lakes and rivers in Tennessee, water activities are also popular. It is the natural and cultural resources, however, that make this a park system of which all Tennesseans can be proud.

This book is not meant to be a comprehensive guide to the parks of Tennessee, but rather a sampling of some of the better- and lesser-known local, state, and national parks that preserve the state's heritage of scenic and natural wonders.

Conservation Note

Radnor Lake is where I work and live. It is also where I seek daily reassurance that there is hope we can preserve and protect mother earth. A park ranger's life is full of the joys our parks can bring and the pressures they must resist, especially on one particular fall day.

November 11, 1993

Today I spotted a young bobcat slip from the thick underbrush near the Hall Farm barn. Bobcats are a rare sighting here, but this was the second one I have seen in the past five days. This cat was stalking birds that fed along the road. With his short tail twitching nervously, he spooked the birds but came up empty-handed. He disappeared into the underbrush as silently as he appeared.

The weather today is in the sixties, and, surprisingly, many of the brilliant fall colors still persist. The lake level is lower than I have ever seen it, yet quite a few waterfowl remain on the lake. The canvasbacks arrived just this week. They are one of my favorite ducks—a regal bird with a dark maroon head. Today is one of those days that make you think nature actually could have a chance in this urban sanctuary.

On the way home from work, where a muddy trail crosses Otter Creek Road near the big slough, I noticed a freshly fallen black willow. The tree had been cut down by one of the lake's newest residents, a beaver. In nearly six years, I have seen only one other beaver at Radnor Lake. This new arrival has been spotted by a number of visitors over the past several months. Most enjoy watching it, but some argue that because it has been cutting trees it has been damaging the area and should be removed. For myself, I welcome the addition of an element of the ecosystem of Otter Creek that has been missing for too long. This beaver has managed to survive the pressures of his urban home for some time since moving in from the Harpeth River, and he appears to have made the lake his home. Maybe he will learn how to live beside us. . . .

Tonight, while on patrol, I saw the beaver. This time he was slumped by the side of the road next to the muddy path he had made—a victim of a vehicle traveling on a road that should not run through a natural area. . . .

The natural world of Radnor Lake, like most parks, faces mounting pressures from our growing society as we seek to recreate in the great outdoors and make a connection with the land. The preservation of parks and their natural resources will not be possible, however, without substantial efforts. Parks are the best inheritance we can leave for future generations. Early Native American cultures left their inheritance, not for their children or grandchildren, but for the seven generations that were to follow. For us to leave the parks as our inheritance for our children is surely a wise and honorable gift. But taking the steps to enable this inheritance to survive to the seventh generation will be a daunting task.

Mike Carlton

Tennessee Wonders

A Pictorial Guide to the Parks

Roan Mountain State Park

There's nothing like vacationing above the clouds! Roan Mountain State Park is used by campers and hikers as a base to explore the surrounding highlands, particularly Roan Mountain, which is ten miles from the park. The area is renowned for its natural rhododendron garden—one of the largest in the world—and for its breathtaking views of the Appalachians.

Fall comes early to Roan Mountain. With an elevation of more than sixty-two hundred feet, it is the highest peak in the Blue Ridge Mountain chain. From its crest, the view of the mountains of North Carolina and Tennessee extends across the horizon in a blaze of autumn color as early as September. The windswept grassy balds are colder here year-round, and the wind is always blowing. Trees at this elevation are shorter and slightly stunted due to the climatic extremes. The peak of Roan Mountain is a harsh but beautiful place; ravens soar in the updrafts from the valleys—a reminder of the wildness of this area. The rhododendron gardens provide a splash of glossy green in the fall, but brilliant pink blossoms carpet the area in the early summer.

Sheltered by Roan Mountain and the Cherokee National Forest, Roan Mountain State Park occupies the lower valley. Grassy meadows and the swift, cold waters of the Doe River present a less severe environment than the mountaintop.

Trillium, orchids, larkspur, and other wildflowers line the banks of the many streams crisscrossing the park. More than 180 different wildflowers have been documented in this area, many of them unique to the region.

Wildlife in the Roan Mountain area is prolific, including more than 150 species of birds. White-tailed deer live in the valleys, and black bears have been seen occasionally. Many species of animals typical of more northerly regions thrive in the cooler climate, including the red squirrel, found only in the mountainous evergreen forests of East Tennessee. The Doe River provides good fishing for rainbow trout when the water level is high.

Roan Mountain State Park offers twenty completely furnished cabins, each accommodating six adults. The park cabins are among the most popular in the state park system and are usually available only with a reservation. A restaurant near the cabin area serves three meals a day during the summer. The two park campgrounds are very popular. Fifty of the one hundred campsites offer electrical and water hookups. Bathhouses and a laundromat are available, and picnic areas and a swimming pool are nearby.

Hiking and cross-country skiing trails provide scenic, peaceful trips through much of the park. Roan Mountain is the only state park in the south

Squirrels

Three species of tree squirrels are found in Tennessee. The red squirrel is found in mountainous eastern sections of the state, where it inhabits pine and hemlock forests. It is a handsome animal, with a rusty red color, and is the smallest of the state's tree squirrels. They are very vociferous creatures, generally heard before seen, with a chattering-like call. The eastern fox squirrel is the state's largest tree squirrel, often weighing up to two pounds. Its fur is a salt-and-pepper color with red and tan sprinkled throughout. The head and tail are a rusty red color, and older animals often have a grizzled white nose. This species is found in West and Middle Tennessee in pine forests and open wood lots. A melanistic or black phase of fox squirrel is occasionally seen. Less common than the gray squirrel, the fox squirrel has a range that overlaps that of the gray squirrel.

Found wherever there are trees with nuts, the gray squirrel is the state's most common and cosmopolitan tree squirrel. Its size is somewhere between that of the fox and the red squirrel, and it is a uniform gray color. Its tail is especially bushy and is bordered with white-tipped hairs. Gray squirrels nest primarily in trees and build large leaf nests that can be seen during winter months scattered throughout mature hardwood forests.

10

that offers cross-country skiing. The three skiing trails total more than eight miles. Seventeen miles of hiking trails, most of which are generally less than four miles long, offer short day-hikes throughout the park. Some venture to the highland peaks, others to the mountain streams and the Doe River. At the top of the Roan High Knob, hikers can join up with the Appalachian Trail at the state line and discover several scenic overlooks of the surrounding mountains.

Take Hwy. 11E east from Johnson City through Eliza-bethton and Hampton to the community of Roan Moun-tain. At Roan Mountain, take Hwy. 143 south. This route goes through the state park to the top of Roan Mountain and the Appalachian Trail.

Roan Mountain State Park
Route 1, Box 50
Roan Mountain, TN 37687
(615) 772-3303

April-June	Excellent trout fishing on the Doe River
Early May	Carter County wildflower tours and bird walks
June	The Rhododendron Festival
September	Roan Mountain Naturalists Rally
October 1	Last sighting of Common Ravens on the high knob
October 15	Fall foliage at peak color
December 15	Cross-country ski trails open relative to measurable snowfall

Bays Mountain Park

Situated near the northern end of Bays Mountain, this park is one of Tennessee's premier nature preserves. The area is centered around the Kingsport reservoir, originally impounded in 1917 to provide water for the city of Kingsport. Today, the forty-four-acre reservoir provides a jewel-like centerpiece for the park and is complemented by a small zoo, nature center, and planetarium—all within the boundaries of a three-thousand-acre natural area. Managed by the city of Kingsport, Bays Mountain Park is within the city limits in southwest Sullivan County.

The park's natural and environmental education area provides a home for many native wildlife species, including white-tailed deer, bobcat, and Wild Turkey. Ruffed Grouse can be heard drumming in the forest, and a resident flock of Canada Geese can be seen year-round on the lake. In the spring, numerous varieties of wildflowers blanket the floors of the rich coves and hardwood forests of the area.

Twenty-five miles of nature trails wind through the predominantly oak and hickory forest and around the lake. Hikers can pick up a trail map at the nature center. Certain roads are open to mountain bikers.

One of the primary functions of Bays Mountain Park is environmental education, and so the nature center houses exhibits and a planetarium with a forty-foot dome and regularly conducts nature programs and planetarium shows. The lower level of the center has a saltwater "touch" pool and aquariums. Barge rides on the lake provide wonderful opportunities to study the aquatic life. The Farmstead Museum, open seasonally and on weekends, houses exhibits on farming during the nineteenth century. The observatory is open some afternoons and evenings; viewing times are posted in the nature center. Picnic areas are sandwiched between the parking lots, and fishing from the dam is permitted for seniors over sixty-five and youngsters under sixteen on Saturday and Monday from 8:30 A.M. to noon.

The area has several exhibits with live animals. The waterfowl aviary and the otter and deer enclosures provide fine vantage points for viewing and photography. Several native species such as the gray wolf are housed near the nature center.

From Interstate 81, take Kingsport Exit 57B to Interstate 181, formerly known as U.S. Hwy. 23. Travel north on I-181 for 4½ miles to Exit 51 (Wilcox Drive); take Wilcox Drive toward Kingsport less than 1 mile to Reservoir Road; take Reservoir Road approximately 3 miles to Bays Mountain Road and follow the road signs. Signs to the park are posted along the entire route from the I-81 exit.

River Otter

A restocking effort in recent years has tried to increase the state's population of river otters, once nearly extinct in Tennessee. Today it is classified as a threatened species.

The river otter is a social animal, usually traveling in groups of two or more, and is well known for its playful antics. It is an outstanding, if sometimes opportunistic, fisherman that feeds primarily on rough fish but also takes game fish, frogs, and crayfish. It is the most aquatic of Tennessee's mustelids, or weasels, and spends most of its time feeding and playing in the water. The river otter is three to four feet long and dark brown. It resembles a beaver but has a more slender body and lacks the broad scaly tail. Larger and lighter colored than the mink, river otters have webbed feet that aid in swimming. Due to their relatively low numbers and secretive personality, otters are rarely sighted in the wild. With time and luck, Tennessee's restocking efforts will bring the otter population back to a level that will allow more frequent sightings.

Bays Mountain Park
853 Bays Mountain Park Road
Kingsport, TN 37660
(615) 229-9447

March-April	Abundant wildflowers in the park; Ruffed Grouse in mating
April	Canada Geese nest and court; white-tailed deer fawns are born
October 16	Fall colors peak; wooly worms in abundance

Great Smoky Mountains National Park

It is hard to imagine a more beautiful place on earth than the Great Smoky Mountains. Waterfalls cascade over moss-covered rocks in more than six hundred miles of streams within the park. Laurel and rhododendron grow lush and thick on the mountains and in the valleys. Giant hemlocks and poplars stand guard over the cove forests; rare and

delicate wildflowers carpet the forest floor and line the winding roads. Tall mountains, enshrouded by mist, reach toward the clouds, and everywhere there is silence—peace and quiet like nowhere else. The Great Smoky Mountains National Park is a true wilderness area; it is also the country's most heavily visited national park. Each year eight million visitors seek out the tranquility and beauty of this five-hundred-thousand-acre preserve.

Clingman's Dome and Newfound Gap are two popular areas in the park near the North Carolina-Tennessee border. Here distant valleys and cloud-covered mountains create one of the most scenic vistas in the entire park. At 6,642 feet, Clingman's Dome is the tallest peak in the park and the second tallest in the eastern United States. The high elevations of these two locations, combined with the breezy mists from the clouds, make this area substantially cooler than the lower valley. The main park road from Gatlinburg, Tennessee, to Cherokee, North Carolina, provides access to the area, but it is frequently closed during the winter months due to snow, ice, or inclement weather.

The Sugarlands Visitors Center is the hub of activity in the Smokies. Natural-history exhibits—featuring images by renowned nature photographer Eliot Porter—interpret the vast expanses and unique features of the area. Programs about the park are shown in the auditorium. The visitors

center also offers an information desk and gift shop. Behind the nature center, easy hiking trails wind through the mountain-stream valley, affording glimpses of Virginia bluebells and long-spurred violets. The park headquarters is directly behind the visitors center and near the Gatlinburg entrance to the park.

The small community of Roaring Fork with tall hemlock trees and clear mountain streams is one of the most beautiful areas in the Smokies. A five-and-a-half-mile nature trail follows an old wagon road that leads to Roaring Fork and provides glimpses of many cascading streams. The trails to

Grotto Falls and Rainbow Falls may be a little strenuous, but reward hikers with breathtaking views of majestic hemlocks and an abundance of colorful wildflowers. Huge moss-covered, dead trees litter the ground beside the trail, the remains of a once-huge American chestnut stand. Rainbow Falls was named for the minirainbow created by the spray floating through the afternoon sunlight into LeConte Creek, eighty feet below.

Open meadows surrounded by tall mountains make Cade's Cove one of the most picturesque settings in the Great Smoky Mountains. A one-way, eleven-mile loop winds through a valley that once

housed the settlement of Cade's Cove, which was settled in the early 1800s. The loop road passes many of the remaining churches and homesteads of the community. Most of these buildings are open to the public and are used to show how settlers once lived in the mountain village. Some agriculture is still practiced in the cove, as evidenced by the cattle and fences in the central valley. One of Cade's Cove's trails leads to twenty-foot-high Abrams Falls. Wildflowers such as mayapple and mountain laurel adorn the five-mile trail to the falls, named for a Cherokee chief who adopted the name Abrams.

Black Bear

Found only in Tennessee's mountainous eastern counties, the black bear is the state's largest surviving native wildlife species. Most bears in the state are found in or near the Great Smoky Mountains and the Cherokee National Forest. Few wildlife sightings trigger more interest than a glimpse of a wild bear. In the Great Smoky Mountains, for example, a bear sighting literally creates a "bearjam," as car after car stops to view the bear. Recent management of the state's bear population to reduce human contact and its association as a food source has reduced bear sightings. These measures have also eliminated many potentially dangerous encounters and returned the bear to the status of wildlife. Visitors to these areas are prohibited from feeding the wildlife.

Black bears are the smallest of the three North American bear species, weighing between two hundred and four hundred pounds and standing up to six feet tall. Since black bears are primarily nocturnal, daytime sightings are unusual. This mammal has a well-developed sense of smell to compensate for its poor eyesight and otherwise average hearing. It is the only species of North American bear that climbs trees, a defensive reaction taken by adults and cubs when danger threatens. Bears by their very nature are secretive and solitary, preferring to feed primarily on plant material, but they are omnivorous and will eat almost anything available to them. These bears go into a semihibernation during the lean winter months, so sightings during this time of year are rare. This is also the time when female bears give birth to their young, one to three cubs weighing from seven to twelve ounces. Babies, born almost hairless, are nursed by their hibernating mother. When the mother awakens from her sleep, the cubs may be two or more months old and may already have opened their eyes. Young bears will stay with their mother for approximately a year, and these mother bears often prove themselves zealous and aggressive in the defense of their young.

During the fall, a mosaic of brilliant reds, oranges, and yellows is splashed against the surrounding mountains. On the weekends of October, when the fall colors are at their peak, the crowds of people visiting Cade's Cove can be very large and can be avoided by visiting on weekdays.

In addition to the cove's historical value and its magnificent scenery, abundant wildlife roams the valley. White-tailed deer feed in the many open meadows of the cove, often seemingly oblivious to people. Groundhogs, raccoons, striped skunks, Wild Turkeys, and coyotes also populate the fields and forests of the cove. Occasionally black bears have been seen venturing to the forest's edge.

The plant life in the Great Smoky Mountains is one of the park's most outstanding features. More than sixteen hundred species of flowering plants have been identified in the region, making it one of the most diverse areas in the country. The range of elevations—from 850 feet in some valleys up to 6,642 feet at Clingman's Dome—provides a variety of different climates and habitats. Many people visit the Smokies from mid-April through May to take in the colorful display of spring flowers. Showy orchids, yellow and pink lady's slippers, yellow and purple fringed orchids, and several species of trillium are just a sample of the rare and delicate plants that make their home in the Smokies. Wildflowers such as columbine, wild geranium, and Dutchman's breeches thrive near the rocky roadsides of Cade's Cove. These, of course, aren't the only show here. Dogwoods and redbuds are some of the earliest blooming trees, from mid- to late April, introducing brilliant splashes of white and

Opossum

Tennessee's only marsupial, the opossum has a ratlike appearance with a naked, prehensile tail that it uses like a fifth limb. The thumbs on its hind feet are opposable, like a human thumb, and nailless, which aid in climbing and grasping. Opossums are about the size of a house cat, whitish gray in color, with a pink pointed nose and thin black ears. These animals are frequently seen along roadsides where they have been struck by cars. They are slow-moving animals that often freeze when caught in the headlights of a car. When an opossum is disturbed, it will hiss and attempt to look threatening. If this stratagem fails, it will play dead, a well-known trait from which the phrase "playing 'possum" is derived. The baby opossum is born naked and

extremely small, weighing only about one-fifteenth of an ounce. An entire litter of newborn opossums can be held in a teaspoon. The young will remain in their mother's pouch and nurse until they are about two months old.

They then begin to hitch rides on their mother's back. Opossums are omnivorous creatures, eating most anything, alive or dead, including carrion. They are primarily nocturnal foragers and are rarely seen during daylight hours.

pink to the otherwise leafless early spring forest. Mountain silverbell, rhododendron, and mountain laurel paint the landscape with color from mid-April through July.

There is also a diversity of wildlife in the Smokies. The heavy annual rainfall makes the moist forests home to more than twenty species of salamanders. The red-cheeked salamander, found at altitudes higher than twenty-eight hundred feet, is found nowhere else in the world. The park is a virtual paradise for bird watchers, as more than two hundred species of birds have been seen here. The high-altitude forests attract birds that are typically found much farther north. Among the more unusual mammals are the river otter, which has been recently reintroduced to the streams of the

area, and the red wolf, which was brought back to the forests.

Many recreational opportunities are available in the Great Smoky Mountains. Cade's Cove is closed to all motor-vehicle traffic on Saturday mornings from early May through mid-September so that bicyclists may enjoy the scenic route through the cove. The area's many streams are open year-round to fishing, and a complete list of regulations, obtainable at the visitors center, provides information regarding specific areas within the park.

Five of ten developed campgrounds are found in the Tennessee portion of the park. Two of the campgrounds in Cade's Cove and Elkmont, open

throughout the year, offer almost 400 campsites. Abrams Creek, a small 16-site campground, and Cosby, a 174-site campground, are open in April. Look Rock, a 92-site campground, opens in mid-May. No trailer hookups or showers are available in these campgrounds.

Mount LeConte Lodge is accessible only by hiking or horse trails, and yet it is so popular that reservations are required, usually far in advance. The park headquarters provides reservation information.

A host of educational and recreational opportunities are offered in the park. The Great Smoky Mountains Institute at Tremont offers programs

ranging from workshops in backpacking and photography to discovery camps for children. The national park, in cooperation with the University of Tennessee, offers the Smoky Mountain Field School, which provides intensive weekend and five-day field courses emphasizing the natural features of the Smokies. Ranger-led programs and activities are also available throughout the area. Information and reservations can be obtained at the visitors center and ranger stations.

The Great Smoky Mountains boast more than eight hundred miles of hiking trails, ranging in difficulty from short walks to extended backpacking trails such as the Appalachian Trail along the North Carolina-Tennessee state line. These trails wind through some of the most rugged and picturesque areas in the continental United States.

Hwy. 441 through Sevierville, Pigeon Forge, and Gatlinburg enters the park at the Great Smoky Mountains National Park Headquarters. This route passes many tourist attractions, dining establishments, and overnight accommodations. For a more scenic, less-hurried route to the Smokies, take Hwy. 321 to Townsend and on to Cade's Cove or the Sugarlands Visitors Center. This route is closed occasionally depending on weather conditions.

Great Smoky Mountains National Park
107 Park Headquarters Road
Gatlinburg, TN 37738
(615) 436-5615

March	Black bears emerge from hibernation; wildflowers starting to blossom
April	Dogwood and redbud trees blossom; trout fishing should be good; initial spring flights of warblers attract bird watchers
Late April	Great Smoky Mountains Wildflower Pilgrimage
June	White-tailed deer and fawns easily viewed at Cade's Cove
October	White-tailed deer bucks jostle for dominance at Cade's Cove
October 15	Fall colors peak

Frozen Head State Park & Natural Area

Frozen Head State Park and Natural Area is a rugged, mountainous area northwest of Knoxville, near Wartburg. Some describe the park as having the scenery of the Great Smoky Mountains without the crowds. There are approximately fourteen peaks that tower more than 3,000 feet within this twelve-thousand-acre natural area. Frozen Head, at 3,324 feet, one of the highest peaks in the Cumberlands, is named for the cap of ice and snow it sometimes wears during the winter months, even at times when the remaining mountains and valleys are not covered by snow.

Scenic vistas from the top of Frozen Head Mountain extend as far as the Great Smoky Mountains on a clear day. Near Peach Orchard Gap, along the lookout-tower trail, a vista has been carved to provide a view of the placid valley to the west. The second-growth forest of oak, beech, and maple is festooned with fall color usually around the third or fourth weekend in October. The spring wildflower assortment is one of Tennessee's most spectacular, with such rare plants as yellow lady's slipper and the bent or nodding trillium. The Panther Branch Trail to Debord and Emory Gap Falls provides a relatively easy walk among these spring wildflowers. The oak forest gives way to hemlock at Debord Falls, a small fifteen-to-twenty-foot waterfall that tumbles into a clear pool at Flat Fork Creek. Below these falls and along Judge Creek

fishermen find rainbow trout, which are stocked by the Tennessee Wildlife Resources Agency. The Panther Gap Rockhouse is a short hike from the lookout-tower trail. More than thirty feet in height in

places, this unique and beautiful geological feature provides shelter from sudden storms. Lush growths of ferns and moss flourish where water has seeped through the limestone. Wildlife is abundant too; it is not unusual to see white-tailed deer and Barred Owls or to hear the distant drumming of Ruffed Grouse.

Frozen Head offers more than fifty miles of hiking and backpacking trails, ranging from easy to strenuous. A color map detailing twelve well-marked trail routes is available at the visitors center. Back-country camping is provided through ten primitive campsites.

Many trails were formerly logging and jeep trails that were cut wide and well maintained. They are,

however, often rocky and steep. Since Frozen Head is a natural area, everything—including the snakes—is protected. Unfortunately for hikers, the extremely rugged, rocky topography of the area provides an ideal habitat for copperheads and rattlesnakes, which hide around logs and rocky areas.

Take the Harriman exit from Interstate 40 to U.S. Hwy. 27 north to Wartburg. From Wartburg, take Hwy. 62 east 2.1 miles to Flat Fork Road, then turn left and travel 4 miles past Morgan County Correctional Institution to the park entrance.

Snakes

Snakes are the most maligned and misunderstood of reptiles. All snakes serve important predatory roles in nature as they feed on a great variety of pests, especially mice and insects. When encountering humans, most snakes would rather retreat than fight, although there are a few exceptions. The black racer, for example, has a peculiar habit of seeming to chase people. This, however, is more a defense mechanism as the racer attempts to stay in sight of danger. Most venomous snakes appear slow to retreat, largely because they are heavy bodied and slow moving. Venom, of course, need not be accompanied by speed once the prey has been bitten.

Snakes are characterized by the absence of limbs, ear openings, and eyelids. Their jaws are expandable to allow them to swallow their prey. Most of the snakes of Tennessee are constrictors, which means they coil around and suffocate their prey. Of the state's more than twenty species of snakes, only four are venomous. These four species are the copperhead, timber rattlesnake, pygmy rattlesnake, and cottonmouth, all of which are pit vipers. Some of the physical characteristics of pit vipers are a generally thicker and heavier body shape, heat-sensing pits behind the nostrils, elliptical pupils, a single row of scales on the bottom of the tail, and a puffy-cheeked appearance caused by the presence of venom sacs.

Timber rattlesnakes are found in dry, rocky areas across the state. A tail rattle and mottled black-and-cream coloration are two easily identified signs. The pygmy rattlesnake, however, is an uncommon sight and appears on the state's threatened-species list. Found mostly in West Tennessee, the pygmy rattler is twelve to eighteen inches in length, and it is the state's smallest pit viper. The copperhead is the state's most widespread venomous snake. It lives in dry upland areas and can be identified by its tan and rusty hourglass markings. The cottonmouth is not found east of the Tennessee River. It is identified by its preferred habitat—water—and its generally belligerent behavior. The cottonmouth does not move quickly to yield to most intruders, including humans. It is dark brown in color with white striping under the chin and a recognizable white interior of its mouth.

Many nonpoisonous species of snakes mimic the cryptic

Timber rattlesnake

Green snake

colorations found in the pit vipers. The red rat, or corn, snake has a checkered pattern with colorations very similar to the copperhead. Water snakes have similar markings, body shape, and temperament to the cottonmouth. Many of the rat snakes rattle their tail in leaves making a sound that is similar to the warning of rattlesnakes. Yet rat snakes are considered a welcome animal around many farms because of the large numbers of mice and rats that they consume. Many people consider king snakes beneficial because they dine on other snakes, including poisonous species.

It is particularly important to note that most snake bites are the result of carelessness. All snakes given a way to retreat will retreat. Attempting to handle snakes is generally a bad idea unless one is experienced. As with all creatures, snakes have their place and should be left alone, particularly in all parks where rules and regulations are designed to protect all the features—including snakes.

Frozen Head State Park and Natural Area
Route 3, Box 321
Wartburg, TN 37887
(615) 346-3318

March-April	Streams are stocked with rainbow trout
April	Spring Wildflower Pilgrimage during second and third weekends
December	Annual Christmas program

Hiwassee Scenic River and Ocoee River

Clear and cold, the Hiwassee is one of East Tennessee's most beautiful rivers, and a stretch of almost twenty-four miles has been designated as a state scenic river. Almost three-quarters of a million acres of forested-mountain watersheds drain from the Chattahoochee, Natahala, and Cherokee national forests to form this Class 1 to Class 3 river. Where the Hiwassee winds out of the foothills and into the valley, the riverbanks are lined with tall sycamore trees.

More than sixty-five species of fish and freshwater mussels are found in the exceptionally clear water of the river. Fishing for rainbow and brown trout and smallmouth bass is often excellent. The water level, however, can fluctuate widely since the flow is controlled by the Tennessee Valley Authority.

Picnic and river-access areas are along State Route 30 on the south side of the river and are managed by Tennessee State Parks. More than twenty miles of hiking trails wind along the river and through the foothills and mountains. These are complemented by several miles of horseback-riding trails.

Information about raft rentals and guided trips is available at the Hiwassee River Office, just off Highway 411, south of the river bridge. Rafting on the Hiwassee is less difficult but as enjoyable as on the Ocoee River.

The Gee Creek Campground is adjacent to the Gee Creek Wilderness Area, part of the Cherokee National Forest. The campground offers forty campsites without hookups but with a bathhouse with showers. Primitive back-country camping is permitted along most of the John Muir State Scenic Trail between Reliance and Coker Creek. This trail traces the famous naturalist's route across the Tennessee wilderness during his thousand-mile walk to the Gulf of Mexico.

The Ocoee River is one of Tennessee's most popular and challenging white-water rivers. With white-water ratings of Classes 1 through 5, it has been chosen as the site of the 1996 Olympic white-water competition. Commercial outfitters lead rafting trips from late March through early November. The surrounding Ocoee River District is part of the 604,000-acre Cherokee National Forest that covers the eastern edge of the state. Twenty-five miles of hiking trails traverse the area's mountainous forests.

Salamanders

These amphibians live in water or under rocks or logs throughout Tennessee. To observe salamanders, you have to go out of your way to find these secretive and genuinely overlooked animals. Although similar in size and body shape to lizards, salamanders can be distinguished from these small reptiles by their smooth, moist skin, which in some species is actually a respiratory organ. Salamanders also lack the clawed toes and visible eardrums present in lizards. Salamanders are completely carnivorous, dining on an assortment of insects and their larva. More than twenty-five species are found statewide, and the Great Smoky Mountains are home to perhaps the greatest diversity of species of salamanders in the world. The respiratory function of the salamanders' skin makes moist locations an important environmental factor in their survival. Identification of salamanders can be a difficult task for the inexperienced naturalist, and in some cases hybridization makes identification even more difficult. Two of the more common families of Tennessee salamanders are the aquatic and lungless salamanders.

Aquatic salamanders spend most or all of their lives in or near water. The hellbender is one of the largest members of this group. More than twenty inches long, it is one of the largest species of salamanders in the world. In many cases aquatic salamanders may have replaced their lungs with gills, and their skin has become an important respiratory organ. Their tail is generally flattened to improve their movement in water. Aquatic salamanders usually lay their eggs in water, although there are some exceptions. Care should be taken when walking in streams, since every rock may be the home of a salamander.

Lungless salamanders can be identified by a large number of coastal grooves—riblike grooves— on their sides. Their bodies are typically long and slender with a round tail. They breathe through their skin and mouth. Eggs are usually suspended beneath moist rocks and logs. Lungless salamanders live primarily in leaf litter and beneath rocks and logs of the eastern deciduous forests. The woodland salamanders are an abundant and widespread genus of salamanders within this group. The slimy salamander is a woodland salamander that has an interesting defense mechanism of secreting a jellylike substance through its skin when it feels threatened. Other salamanders in this family include dusky, brook, zigzag, and cave salamanders.

Winter Waterfowl

More than twenty-five species of ducks and geese winter on Tennessee lakes and rivers, providing one of nature's true spectacles when they congregate.

Three species of geese are found in Tennessee. Canada Geese, the most common, can be found statewide. Snow and White-fronted Geese are infrequent visitors, more often seen in West Tennessee. Their long necks and comparatively large body size make them easy to distinguish between geese and ducks.

Ducks fall into two distinct groups: dabbling (or puddle) ducks and diving ducks. Dabbling ducks are found around shallow, sheltered bodies of water; diving ducks are more often found near deep water. Dabblers are tip-up feeders, that is,

they do not completely submerge when they feed. Divers live up to their name, submerging completely when feeding. An iridescent speculum, or colored wing patch, is found only on a dabbling duck. Dabblers spring into the air on takeoff, whereas divers patter along the surface of the water until they gain altitude. The most commonly seen dabblers are the Mallard, Gadwall, American Wigeon, American Black Duck, pintail, and teal. The most common diving ducks are the Ring-necked Duck, Lesser Scaup,

Bufflehead, Canvasback, and Common Goldeneye.

Mergansers are ducklike birds that can often be found accompanying wintering ducks. They are fish-eating birds, often referred to as fish ducks. Their narrow, serrated bills allow them to grasp fish easily and provide bird watchers with a convenient field sign for all mergansers. Three species occur infrequently in Tennessee: the Hooded Merganser, Common Merganser, and the Red-breasted Merganser.

Although the Wood Duck is sometimes lumped with puddle ducks, its behavior differs and includes perching in trees. Wood Ducks are easily identified by their multiple colors and the adult male's distinct markings. Most resident Wood Ducks flock together in late September to migrate south, although some birds remain year-round.

Take Hwy. 411 to Etowah and Benton. The visitors center is southwest of the Hiwassee River Bridge.

Hiwassee State Scenic River
Box 255
Delano, TN 37325
(615) 263-1341

Take U.S. Hwy. 64 to Cleveland.

Ocoee Ranger District
Route 1, Parksville
Benton, TN 37307

March-April	Ocoee River runs only on weekends
April-May	Brown and rainbow trout fishing excellent on the Hiwassee
May-September	Ocoee runs five days per week
September-November	Ocoee runs only on weekends
November	Flocks of Ring-necked Ducks begin to appear on the Hiwassee

Big South Fork and Pickett State Park

The quiet is impressive to hikers in the dense forests of the Big South Fork, the only sounds being those of nature. Rushing streams pass under huge rock overhangs where the Cumberland Plateau gives way to deep rocky gorges. Very little of this land of the Upper Cumberland has anything to do with man-made creations. It is easy to see why John Muir felt these forests were "impressively solitary." The John Muir Trail that winds through the area is a subtle reminder that the naturalist traveled past the Tennessee wilderness on his thousand-mile walk to the gulf.

This area was once heavily invaded by timber and mining interests, but recent conservation efforts have helped the area to recover and become one of the premier wild and scenic sites in the eastern United States. Pickett State Park and Big South Fork combine to form the largest preserved area on the Cumberland Plateau.

The area's streams and rivers have cut deep gorges in the plateau, and many of these features, particularly the overhangs, were sites for prehistoric habitation by Native Americans. More recently, they harbored moonshiners' stills. One of the area's most outstanding park sites is the Twin or Double Arches, seven-tenths of a mile from the Twin Arches trail head. The largest of the arches is approximately seventy feet high and more than a hundred feet wide; the other arch is slightly smaller, around fifty feet high and nearly a hundred feet wide.

The roadways do not offer the best views of the area. Hiking is the only way to really appreciate the Big South Fork, and there are two hundred miles of trails for doing that. Well-marked overnight backpacking paths such as the Sheltowhee Trace and the John Muir Trail meander through the gorges and along the top of the plateau, revealing many old homesteads and postcard-perfect natural wonders.

The plant and animal life are typical of the Cumberland Plateau. Abundant patches of rare plants, such as yellow lady's slippers, are scattered throughout the forest. More than a hundred species of birds and fifty species of mammals regard this area as home at various times during the year. Big-leafed magnolias, with some leaves as long as three feet, can be found in the gorges. Canadian hemlock and rhododendron line the gorges, and the plateau top is covered with mast——or nut——producing trees such as oak and hickory. It is hoped that, as these trees mature, an

Striped Skunk

The striped skunk, a common and often unwanted wildlife species, is Tennessee's most prevalent skunk. (The spotted skunk is smaller and seldom seen.) Skunks are well known for their ability to spray powerful and persistent musk onto would-be predators. The characteristic white stripe on the black body of the striped skunk is widely recognized as a warning sign to give this animal a wide berth. This species is roughly the size of a house cat. The Great Horned Owl is just about the only predator that will take skunks. Like many birds, the Great Horned Owl has very little or no sense of smell, a real advantage when preying on skunks. The striped skunk is seen primarily at night when it forages for insects, berries, and small animals.

Many parks throughout the state now have quite healthy striped skunk populations. Campers often glimpse them in the evening as the animals forage for scraps of food. Common sense is the only defense in any encounter with a skunk. Never threaten or surprise it, and don't leave food out. If watched with caution, a skunk can prove to be interesting. Skunks can, however, be carriers of rabies. Should a skunk appear sick, it should be scrupulously avoided.

abundance of nuts will encourage the reintroduction of black bears into the area.

Big South Fork is a national river and recreation area straddling the border of Tennessee and Kentucky. In Tennessee, Bandy Creek offers a visitors center, modern camping facilities, a swimming pool, and horseback-riding stables. Areas for swimming, boating, and fishing can be found at seven locations along the Big South Fork and its tributaries: Clear Fork, North White Oak, and the New River. Hunting is open throughout the area, except in designated safety zones. The Charit Creek Lodge provides back-country lodging. Mountain biking and horseback riding are allowed on more than a hundred miles of the trail system. Reservations, maps, and other information are available at the Bandy Creek Visitors Center.

Pickett State Park adjoins the western boundary of the Big South Fork. Its nearly twelve thousand acres include some of Tennessee's most scenic natural and geological wonders. This part of the Cumberland Plateau boasts deep, shadowy gorges carved by cool mountain streams and some of the most unusual wildflowers and plant life found outside the Great Smoky Mountains National Park. Big-leafed magnolia, Canadian hemlock, and rhododendron are abundant. The area also possesses several natural bridges carved from the

plateau's sandstone. The park has more than fifty miles of hiking trails past waterfalls, caves, and sheer bluffs. Hazard Cave has one of the area's best-recognized sights. Towering more than fifty feet, the multilevel Hazard Cave displays many layers of colorful sandstone.

White-tailed deer and Wild Turkey are common in the park, with signs of wild boar evident throughout the forest. The small fifteen-acre Arch Lake is a popular spot for trout fishing. Most of the area is devoted to wildlife management.

Land for the park was deeded to the state in 1933 by the Sterns Coal and Lumber Company. With assistance from the National Park Service and the Civilian Conservation Corps, trails, cabins, picnic areas, the lake, and other recreational facilities were developed.

Today the facilities within Pickett State Park welcome a wide spectrum of visitors. The chalets—five wooden-and-stone cabins—offer some of Tennessee's most popular state park weekend getaways. Five rustic stone cabins and five wooden cabins are also available. The sandy beach is surrounded by tall sandstone cliffs and is open seasonally. A boat dock at Arch Lake rents canoes and rowboats, and a group camp is open to larger parties. A forty-site campground, situated in a forest setting, has electrical and water hookups at thirty-one sites. Picnicking and playground sites are scattered throughout the developed sections of the park.

For Big South Fork Natural River and Recreation Area, from Hwy. 127 at Jamestown, go east on Hwy. 154 to Hwy. 297. From Oneida, go west on Hwy. 297. Hwy. 297 crosses through the southern end of the area and provides access to the Bandy Creek Visitors Center and Scott State Forest. For Pickett State Park, from I-40 take U.S. Hwy. 127 north to Jamestown to State Route 154 to the park entrance.

Great Horned Owl

The Great Horned Owl is the largest of Tennessee's owls. An aggressive predator, it is one of the very few animals that will prey on a skunk. Large ear tufts and bright yellow eyes are two identifying characteristics for individuals fortunate enough to glimpse this bird in the wild. Primarily a nocturnal hunter, the Great Horned Owl is rarely seen yet often heard. Its deep four-to-seven-note call, heard in many wooded areas after sunset, is softer and more muffled than that of the Barred Owl. Great Horned Owls and other birds of prey can often be located during daylight hours by noting the activity of crows, which mob and harass all birds of prey.

Great Horned Owls often nest in the cavities of trees or abandoned nests of other wildlife, such as the Red-tailed Hawk, American Crow, and gray squirrel. The earliest nesting of Tennessee's birds, this owl is sometimes seen covered with snow while incubating during the January-to-March nesting season. Great Horned Owls defend their nests and territories aggressively and have been known to attack interlopers who get too close to a nest. Accordingly, the Great Horned Owl's nickname is the "tiger of the sky."

**Big South Fork National River
and Recreation Area**
Route 3, Box 401
Oneida, TN 37841
Bandy Creek Visitors Center: (615) 879-3625 or (615) 429-5704
Park Headquarters: (615) 569-9778

Pickett State Park
Polk Creek Route
Box 174
Jamestown, TN 38556
(615) 879-5821

January	Great Horned Owls begin to nest
March-April	Rainbow trout stocked in Arch Lake
April-May	Wildflowers blossom
May-June	Mountain laurel and rhododendron blossom in the area gorges
October 15	Autumn colors peak

South Cumberland Recreational Area

Seven natural areas and parks at the southern end of the Cumberland Plateau make up what is collectively called South Cumberland State Park. Comprising almost twelve thousand acres, it is one of the few remaining wildernesses in Tennessee. A wide assortment of natural and geological features underlines the scenic aspect of the park, including huge tulip poplar trees that line the many gulfs and gorges. Stands of oak and pine cover the plateau, and carpets of spring wildflowers connect the gulfs with brilliant splashes of color. In the late winter and early spring, the region is dotted with hundreds of ephemeral waterfalls cascading into the gulfs from wet-weather springs in the sides of the bluffs and from the plateau top. In the fall, the bright yellow of the poplars and the crimson of the sweet gum trees set the landscape aflame with color.

The main visitors center is on Highway 56, between Monteagle and Tracy City. It houses exhibits about the cultural and natural history of the locality and provides information and maps on the many park trails. Picnic and recreation sites are nearby. All parts of the South Cumberland State Park are accessible from Interstate 24 at Monteagle.

The Sewanee Natural Bridge State Natural Area is a small, two-acre plot that features a twenty-five-foot-high natural sandstone arch that is flat on top and can be walked over. It is reached by a short trail from the parking lot. A small wet-weather spring trickles from a rock house adjacent to the arch. Overlooking scenic Lost Cove, the natural area is 2.3 miles south of Sewanee on Highway 56.

Carter State Natural Area, situated at the source of Crow Creek in Lost Cove, is a 140-acre site donated to the state in 1976 by Mr. and Mrs. Harry Lee Carter. Its most impressive feature is Buggytop Cave, deep within which is the celebrated Honeymoon Passage. There it is said a young couple once spent their wedding night to avoid a shivaree, a traditional southern noisy serenade of newlyweds. The entrance to the cave, sheltered by 150-foot-high bluffs, measures more than 100 feet wide and 30 feet high. It is reached down a two-mile trail that parallels Highway 56. The parking area for the site is a pull-off on Highway 56, approximately five miles south of Sewanee. The cave is open to the public, and guided tours are sometimes available from the staff of naturalists at the visitors center.

One of South Cumberland State Park's most scenic areas is a small Tennessee Valley Authority wild area called Foster Falls, a majestic sixty-foot-high waterfall that creates a powerful water flow throughout most of the year. Sheer two-hundred-foot-high cliffs line the bowl surrounding the falls. The area is a popular rock-climbing venue,

although most of the good climbs are on private property. The falls mark the southern end of the Fiery Gizzard Trail. A picnic shelter and tables are near the parking area, and a small campground without hookups is open seasonally. Foster Falls is approximately seven miles south of Tracy City, on Highway 150 on a well-marked route.

The Fiery Gizzard Trail extends south from the 212-acre Grundy Forest State Natural Area. This thirteen-mile trail winds along the east side of Fiery Gizzard Gulf and Creek, one of Tennessee's most rugged and scenic areas. Trillium, dwarf crested iris, and other wildflowers grow prolifically in this area. Several campsites line the route, but most of the land around the trail is privately owned.

Several stories purport to explain how Fiery Gizzard Creek and Fiery Gizzard Trail were named. One draws on the proximity of coke ovens, and another claims that whiskey made from the creek caused a "mighty fire in the gizzard." The most colorful story relates to the legendary woodsman Davy Crockett, who lived there at one time. Legend has it that one day he was having no luck while hunting and his pride prevented him from seeking food from other people. Finally he came across a hunting camp at the head of a creek, where a friendly group offered him food cooking over their campfire. Crockett plunged his knife into the meat, cut a piece, and swallowed it, ignoring the temperature of the food except to exclaim, "Damn, that's a mighty fiery gizzard," thereby naming the creek.

Grundy Lakes State Park offers many diversions, including a beach and swimming area, picnic sites, and hiking trails. Fishing in the clear waters of the four Grundy lakes can yield catches of bluegill, catfish, and bass. The area is also the home of the Lone Rock Coke ovens, where coal was converted to coke in the late 1800s using convict labor. The park is northeast of Tracy City. From the second traffic light, follow the signs; the route is well marked.

Wood Duck

Few creatures possess the rainbow of colors the male Wood Duck sports in its breeding plumage. A medium-sized duck, the male has an iridescent green head with white striping and a white chin. The bill is orange, yellow, and white; and the eyes are red. The Wood Duck's chest is chestnut colored with white spots, and its body and wings are covered with green, purple, and blue iridescent feathers. The female is inconspicuously colored but possesses an obvious white eye ring. One of Tennessee's most common nesting species, the duck population at one time suffered a dearth of nesting sites. Today, through the introduction of nesting boxes, the Wood Duck has rebounded and is now a common sight along waterways during the spring, summer, and fall. In September, large flocks form in preparation for migrating flights south.

The Savage Gulf State Natural Area is the largest and perhaps the most spectacular section of the South Cumberland State Park. It was named for an early settler, but the adjective *savage* is an accurate description. More than fifty miles of hiking trails and ten primitive campsites make this area especially popular with backpackers and hikers. Seven major waterfalls are found along the trail system, and the plateau's flat top conceals the eight-hundred-foot-deep gulfs of Savage Creek, the Collins River, and Big Creek. The limestone and shale base of these gulfs allows the rivers to disappear and then reappear at another location. Both the Collins River and Big Creek flow underground for some distance. The Stone Door and Savage Gulf ranger stations provide entrances to the natural area.

Horse Pound Falls in Savage Gulf derived its name from the natural enclosure formed by the falls and the surrounding gulf, which enabled early settlers to corral their horses without having to erect fences. During the Civil War, many entrepreneurs stole horses and sold them to both sides while hiding the horses in the gorge.

The Stone Door Ranger Station received its name from the Great Stone Door, a 150-foot natural passageway that drops through the western crown of the plateau above Big Creek. The overlook there offers scenic vistas of the gulfs, which are shaped like a bird's foot, and is reached by a short, paved trail. Great Stone Door is the western access point to the backpacking trail system and is the South Cumberland's only designated rappelling and climbing site owned by the state. Primitive campsites are found near the ranger station and at several points along the trails. Trail maps are available at the Stone Door Ranger Station, east of Beersheba Springs, off Highway 56.

The Savage Gulf Ranger Station sits atop the eastern edge of Savage Gulf. Access to this area's many scenic wonders is strictly by hiking trail.

Warblers

Warblers are one of the most challenging, yet rewarding, families of songbirds to observe in the spring and fall; more than thirty-five species have been documented in Tennessee. Of these, as many as twenty-four species nest in the state. Their quick and constant motion in search of insects in thick vegetation is characteristic of these birds. Drab-colored fall warblers are easily confused with immature birds, as the males molt their brilliant breeding colors and are justifiably referred to as "confusing fall warblers." The spring plumage of male warblers offers a pleasant surprise to the birder unfamiliar with the species' many bright colors and patterns. The distinctive colors and markings of the males make spring identification of warblers easier, but their constant motion may encourage birders to identify them by their varied songs instead. Warbler watching has almost risen to the level of a sport, as many birders pride themselves on the number of different species they can count on an outing. Warbler watching is possible in most regions of the state, as these neotropical migrants pass through Tennessee when traveling to and from their Central American wintering grounds.

From the parking area, a four-mile loop trail leads to the Savage Falls overlook, revealing the cascades and thirty-foot falls. The relatively level South Rim Trail winds along the southern rim of Savage Gulf, where numerous overlooks provide scenic views of outstanding natural features, including one of the last remaining stands of virgin timber in the eastern United States. This trail connects to Stagecoach Road, a McMinnville-to-Chattanooga stagecoach toll road that was constructed in the 1830s with slave labor.

From Stagecoach Road, a connecting trail links the east trail system to the trails of Big Creek and Stone Door. Also connecting with Stagecoach Road is the Collins Gulf Trail. This ten-mile loop goes past Horse Pound Falls and Fall Creek Sink, where the Collins River disappears underground, and along the crest of the Collins Gulf. The lengthy Collins Gulf Trail enters one of the most secluded patches of wilderness in Middle Tennessee. The North Rim Trail provides access to Hobbs Cabin, a popular destination for backpackers. The 244-acre Hawkins Cove Natural Area was established in 1985 to protect a rare plant called the Cumberland rosin-weed. This area has not yet been developed for public use.

To reach the Savage Gulf Ranger Station, take Highway 56 north of Tracy City to Highway 108 in Gruetli Laager, and then take Highway 399 to the ranger station. The route is well marked.

South Cumberland State Park
Route 1, Box 2196
Monteagle, TN 37356
Visitors Center (615) 924-2980
Savage Gulf Ranger Station (615) 949-3592

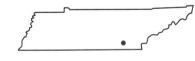

February-March	Numerous seasonal waterfalls caused by late winter rainfall
March-April	Wildflowers blossom
September	Migration of Black and Turkey Vultures
October 16-21	Peak time for fall colors of oak, maple, poplar, and sweet gum

Fall Creek Falls State Park

Waterfalls, cascades, streams, gorges, timberland, and a wide assortment of recreational opportunities—fishing, swimming, hiking, camping, golf, bicycling, horseback riding, tennis, basketball . . . No wonder Fall Creek Falls State Park is one of the most popular resort parks in the Southeast.

While most of this recreational area's more than sixteen thousand acres are oak and hickory forests, tall stands of hemlock surround the sheer two-hundred-foot bluffs that line the gorges. The waterfalls, however, are what set this landscape apart from the other parks of Tennessee.

The most spectacular of the park's five waterfalls is Fall Creek Falls, which tumbles 256 feet into the Cane Creek Gorge to make it the highest waterfall in the eastern United States. Immediately to the right of it a smaller fall flows from Coon Creek. Both are easily accessible from the roadway, and a short walk to the overlook rewards the visitor with a spectacular view of both falls and the gorge.

The nearby road leads to Buzzard's Roost, a scenic two-hundred-foot-high rock outcropping that offers one of the best views of the gorge, and then to Piney Creek Falls. The waterfall and cascades are picturesquely framed by a stand of hemlock at the overlook. Farther down the trail, a swinging bridge crosses Piney Creek.

Cane Creek Falls and Cascade are downstream from the other falls, near the north entrance to the park. The waters of Fall Creek, Piney Creek, and Cane Creek unite to make this 85-foot-high waterfall the largest falls in the park in terms of volume. Rockhouse Falls is a narrow 125-foot waterfall that empties into the same basin as Cane Creek Falls. The best route to these falls is via the trail from the nature center.

The lake is the center of activities for this most-developed resort in the state park system. Fall Creek Falls Inn has seventy-two guest rooms, each with its own balcony or porch overlooking Fall Creek Lake, and it also offers suites, meeting and banquet rooms, a swimming pool, an exercise and fitness room, and a recreation room. The restaurant provides a spectacular view of the lake.

Twenty cabins, each containing two bedrooms, are adjacent to the inn complex. Completely furnished, each can accommodate eight adults. Ten fishing cabins have private porches that extend over the lake, allowing campers to fish from their back doors. The cabins on the land side rise up a wooded hill just above the inn, with patios, picnic tables, grills, playgrounds, and access to the bike trail. Two group lodges near the inn can provide

Fall Creek Falls

Piney Falls

housing for more than a hundred people. The overnight resort facilities at Fall Creek Falls are extremely popular, and reservations are booked up to a year in advance.

For true outdoorspeople, two group camps feature rustic bunkhouses clustered around a central dining room, a bathhouse, and a recreation hall. Three campgrounds contain 227 campsites with electrical and water hookups at every site. Each campground provides bathhouses. All spaces are usually filled on holiday weekends.

For golfers, an eighteen-hole par-72 championship golf course is across the lake from the inn. One of the most beautiful and challenging public golf courses in the country, it was named as one of *Golf Digest*'s top twenty-five public courses.

White-tailed Deer

Tennessee's most-common large mammal is the white-tailed deer. According to recent estimates, more than one-half million deer currently roam the state, where they can be seen in all but the most heavily developed areas. Most Tennessee parks boast at least a few deer, which quickly become accustomed to human contact and can be observed if not approached too closely.

In Tennessee, the white-tailed deer stands approximately three feet tall at the shoulders and weighs between 100 and 150 pounds. The winter coat, displayed from October to April, is coarse and grayish brown in color. The summer coat, shorter and sleeker, is a reddish tan.

The male, or buck, has symmetrical antlers that branch from a single main stem. Antler growth usually begins in April, and the velvet, or summer, antler covering is shed in September, revealing the bony portion of the antler. Antlers are used to establish breeding dominance; as long as a buck is engaged in mating or breeding, its antlers remain attached. As winter draws to a close and the breeding season concludes, usually no later than February, the antlers drop.

The female, or doe, is smaller in size and usually does not have antlers. In April, does become secretive and begin to give birth to their fawns. Twins are not uncommon among healthy deer herds. At this time of the year, many people make the mistake of assuming that a discovered fawn has been abandoned. In most cases, the doe is nearby, anxiously waiting for the intruder to leave.

During its first months of life, the fawn's only defense is its spotted camouflage coloring. As summer arrives, the doe and her fawns begin to venture out to the edges of fields and lakes, never far from safety. Fawns are most visible during these summer months. By September, most fawns have lost their spots and taken on the appearance of adult deer, although generally smaller in size. Fawns will usually stay with their mothers as a family until the next offspring are born the following spring.

Cane Creek Falls

The park headquarters is in the Village Green Complex, the center of all park activities. The complex contains a camp store, laundromat, craft center, and information center. Several recreational facilities surround the complex, including a swimming pool, bathhouse, snack bar, tennis courts, amphitheater, picnic areas, recreation lodge, and ball fields.

The boat dock at Fall Creek Lake offers rental canoes, pedal boats, and fishing boats with electric trolling motors. The lake boasts some of the best fishing in the Tennessee State Park System, with established state records in channel catfish at forty-one pounds and bluegill at three pounds.

One of the best ways to enjoy Fall Creek Falls is to take advantage of its wide variety of trails. There are four miles of horseback-riding trails and a rental stable. A three-mile bike trail follows the lake and ventures through the forest to the high falls. Bikes can be rented at the camper check-in station. Approximately thirty miles of hiking trails traverse the wooded plateau and gorges of the area. In addition, several back-country trails trace the Cane Creek watershed. The lower loop of the trail, twelve miles long, has two campsites and passes the area's three main waterfalls. Several short hiking trails can be found near the nature center and the inn complex.

Turtles

Turtles are an easily recognized reptile. They hibernate during the winter months, burrowing into stream and lake banks as cold weather arrives and not reappearing until the warm sun of spring returns.

Most of Tennessee's ten species of turtles are found in or around water. Snapping and soft-shelled turtles rarely venture out of the water except to lay their eggs and,

Snapping turtle

in the case of snappers, occasionally to sun themselves. The alligator snapper, found in West Tennessee, is the state's largest freshwater turtle, with some specimens weighing in excess of a hundred pounds. The remainder of the state's turtles, sliders in particular, are regularly seen basking in the sun on logs and rocks in order to regulate their body temperature and to rid themselves of unwanted hitchhikers, such as leeches. Aquatic turtles usually have webbed toes and special adaptations that allow them to stay submerged for long periods of time. In some aquatic species, breathing is assisted by the skin of the mouth and cloaca, which are capable of absorbing oxygen from the water much like the gills of a fish.

The box turtle is the state's most commonly encountered

Eastern box turtle

terrestrial turtle, often seen crossing roadways from one wooded area to another. Found statewide in most deciduous forests, it differs from aquatic turtles in that its shell is less flat and its legs are stubbier and better adapted to overland travel. Box turtles are primarily vegetarian feeders, although they will eat earthworms and insects. The box turtle has a hinged shell on its belly that allows it to withdraw completely into its protective shell.

Fall Creek Falls

The park's plant and animal life resemble those found in southern Canada. Wildflowers such as trout lily and spring beauties grow profusely, with the peak viewing time falling between mid-April and early May. In the late summer, bright red cardinal flowers line the banks of Fall Creek Lake close to the bike trail. White-tailed deer roam throughout the park, especially around the golf course and the inn. Canada Geese are year-round residents and quite common around the inn. Wood Ducks can also be seen during the summer in large numbers.

From Cookeville, take Hwy. 111 south to Spencer. From McMinnville, take Hwy. 30 east to Spencer. From Spencer, follow the signs to the north or south entrance to the park. From Pikeville, take Hwy. 127 north to Hwy. 30, then west to the park's north entrance.

Fall Creek Falls State Park
Route 3
Pikeville, TN 37367
Park Headquarters (615) 881-3297
Fall Creek Inn (615) 881-3241

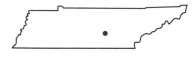

February-March	Waterfalls at their highest flow because of late winter rains
March-May	Wildflowers at their peak
May-June	Excellent largemouth bass and bluegill fishing on the lake
July-August	Channel catfish feeding en masse at night on the lake
September 21	Migrating Broad-winged Hawks seen at the fire tower
October 15	Fall colors peak

Burgess Falls State Natural Area

The three-quarter-mile trail at Burgess Falls State Natural Area follows the course of the Falling Water River. Tumbling from Burgess Falls Lake, the water cascades over a series of beautiful waterfalls and into pools that feed the upper section of the Falling Water Gorge. Moss and watercress are thick everywhere.

These small falls, however, only hint at what the gorge holds in store. Less than a half-mile down the trail, the roaring sound of a much larger waterfall can be heard in the distance. After a series of turns, the river drops more than fifty feet into a limestone bowl with surrounding walls more than a hundred feet high. Many people assume that this is Burgess Falls, because it is so rugged and so powerful.

Those who know trek farther down the trail toward the roar of another waterfall filling the air. At the end of the trail the river becomes a torrent as it squeezes through the narrow gorge, becoming Burgess Falls. Limestone bluffs, some towering more than 200 feet high, line the bowl of these falls. The Falling Water River drops vertically from the bluffs, 130 feet into a pool below. In all, it descends almost 250 feet in less than a mile through the Falling Water River Gorge, a majestic sight of nature.

Burgess Falls had seen many changes before its designation as a natural area. The region was named after Tom Burgess, a Revolutionary War soldier who was deeded the land as payment for his war service. In the early 1920s, the city of Cookeville impounded the river to provide electricity. That use ended in 1944 with the development of hydroelectric projects by the Tennessee Valley Authority. Cookeville deeded the site to the state, and in 1973 it was designated one of Tennessee's first natural areas. The industrial use of the region has left its mark, but time and nature are reclaiming one of the state's truly magnificent natural treasures.

A picnic area adjoins the main parking lot. Fishing is allowed on the lake and on the river below the falls, where Center Hill Lake begins. Both areas are known for excellent fishing.

From Interstate 40, take the Burgess Falls exit south 4.8 miles, then take a left turn at the fork in the road. Travel 1 mile to another left turn. Travel another 2.6 miles to the bridge across Burgess Falls Lake. The park entrance is immediately on the right after crossing the bridge.

Red-tailed Hawk

The Red-tailed Hawk is Tennessee's most commonly seen bird of prey. Observant motorists traveling along any interstate highway will often see this large buteo on a lofty perch surveying the roadsides for an easy meal. It is also often found along open fields and the edges of wooded areas. During winter months, red-tails are frequently seen as they migrate in search of food. The hawk's primary food source is woodland and meadow animals such as rabbits, mice, and even snakes. Its broad wings and tail facilitate the characteristic soaring flight for which it is well known. A rusty red tail indicates an adult bird—an especially obvious field sign when the bird is soaring on a sunny day. The back and head of the red-tail are dark brown, and the chest is light tan with a mottled-brown V-shaped stripe across the abdomen. Red-tails flying high

overhead frequently scream when they encounter other red-tails or are disturbed by crows and other birds.

Pileated Woodpecker

The Pileated Woodpecker is the largest of Tennessee's woodpeckers. Found in wooded areas throughout the state, it is rarely confused with any other species of bird. Almost completely black in color and crow sized, it is occasionally mistaken for an Ivory-Billed woodpecker, which is considered extinct in the United States and has a conspicuous white bill and white on its wings. The Pileated Woodpecker can be distinguished from crows by its red crest and its irregular flapping flight pattern. Males have designated drumming trees from which they emit loud, hollow, hammering sounds; houses can be appealing substitutes for drumming trees. The Pileated Woodpecker's call is a series of high-pitched *cah's.*

Burgess Falls State Natural Area
Route 6, Burgess Falls Road
Sparta, TN 38583
(615) 761-3338

March-April	Waterfalls have greatest water flow of the year
April	Wildflowers begin to bloom
September	Autumn wildflowers in peak
October 21	Autumn colors of beech and maple trees peak

67

Cumberland Mountain State Park

The Cumberland Homestead Project on the Cumberland Plateau has been termed the "Showplace of the New Deal." Part of President Franklin D. Roosevelt's larger scheme to grant subsistence living for the nation's communities stranded by the Great Depression, it provided more than 250 families with homes, seed and equipment to raise agricultural products, and recreational facilities. Its legacy is the Cumberland Mountain State Park.

The Farm Security Administration, founded in 1937, created the recreational park. The construction was provided by the Civilian Conservation Corps (CCC) and the Works Progress Administration (WPA), which gave jobs to the unemployed.

Many park buildings were constructed using a colorful, indigenous sandstone, called Crab Orchard stone, found along the plateau in layers that make it easy to use in construction. It is still a popular building material, and its marketing is an important industry in the area.

Byrd Lake is a narrow strip of water impounded by one of the CCC's largest masonry projects. The facilities include a visitors center, Olympic-size swimming pool, canoes, fishing, paddle boats, picnic areas, tennis courts, recreation lodge, softball fields, and playgrounds. Fishing for bluegill and bass on scenic Byrd Lake is popular, and camping at the park's 150-site campground makes this one of the most popular state parks. Thirty-seven rustic and modern cabins near Byrd Lake are favorite vacation retreats, and the restaurant overlooking the lake is on a par with the best in the state park system.

Ozone Falls State Natural Area is also under the management of Cumberland Mountain State Park. The area is named for the breathtaking 110-foot waterfall where Fall Creek plunges into the gorge below. The view from atop the falls looking west down the gorge is one of most striking vistas in all the state parks. The surrounding woodlands are old-growth forests, and the gorge is lined with huge hemlocks and rhododendron. Large boulders and a clear pool at the base of the falls add to the site's natural beauty. The name *ozone* comes from the small community at the top of the falls, dubbed so because of the local assessment of the "stimulating quality" of the air around the community.

From Interstate 40, take the Peavine Road exit south through Crossville approximately fifteen minutes to the park entrance. The route to the park is well marked. To get to Ozone Falls, from Interstate 40 take the Crab Orchard exit at Hwy. 70, and take Hwy. 70 east 4.6 miles. A small parking area is just west of the Fall Creek Bridge. The falls are a short, easy hike from the parking area.

Coyote

Although it is not a native of the state, the coyote is Tennessee's most common large predator, and its range encompasses virtually the entire state. The loss of large predators native to Tennessee, such as the eastern cougar, red wolf, and black bear, has left a vacancy for a top-level predator to fill. Lacking serious competition, the coyote has moved in with remarkable success.

How the coyote first came to Tennessee is a matter of speculation. Some stories suggest that they were brought in by fox hunters for the purpose of training their dogs. Other accounts have the western coyote hybridizing with domestic dogs to form a sort of supercoyote or "coydog." They may also have previously existed in the northeast-

ern United States and migrated south from that region. The coyote is a crafty and adaptable predator and has expanded its range and numbers in spite of extensive predator control measures.

The eastern coyote is larger than its western counterpart, and its behavior is different. They appear more social, often living and hunting in groups. They are also less vocal. Very few animals can be mistaken for a coyote. The red wolf is slightly larger and runs with its tail

in the air, while the coyote runs with its tail between its legs. The red wolf, however, has a limited range in Tennessee and only very recently was reintroduced into the Great Smoky Mountains. It will likely be many years before the red wolf is observable with any regularity. The coyote's coat, usually a brownish gray, blends perfectly with the colors of the eastern deciduous forests. The red and gray fox are substantially smaller in size, weighing between seven and fifteen pounds, whereas the coyote may weigh between twenty and fifty pounds. Domestic dogs with a shepherd mix can be confused with coyotes if they have gone feral. The footprints of the coyote look like the tracks of a domestic dog, though they are usually a bit more elongated.

Mink

The mink is Tennessee's most common aquatic weasel, but it is rarely seen. Sightings usually occur at sunrise or sunset near water. The mink, a relative of the skunk, has musk glands that, while not capable of spraying, produce a powerful odor. Curiously, mink coats are a women's fashion statement despite the literal translation of the Swedish word *menk,* "the stinking animal from Finland."

Minks are chocolate brown in color; adult males weigh up to four pounds and females weigh slightly less. Their preferred habitat is along waterways that support fish and small mammals. A mink is a constantly moving bundle of energy that is sometimes utterly oblivious to its surroundings.

Cumberland Mountain State Park
Route 8, Box 330
Crossville, TN 38555
(615) 484-6138

March 15	Fragrant trailing arbutus and other spring wildflowers begin to blossom
April 15-June 1	Excellent fishing on Byrd Lake before summer aquatic plants make fishing more difficult
May 20	Mountain laurel begin to blossom
June 20	Pink-flowered rhododendron at their peak
October 19	Fall colors of maple and sweet gum at their peak

Percy and Edwin Warner Parks

In January 1927, Col. Luke Lea donated 868 acres for one of Tennessee's earliest and largest city parks. Lea, a onetime U.S. senator, was encouraged by his father-in-law, Percy Warner, to initiate an effort to establish a nature park close to Nashville. Warner died later that year, and at Lea's urging the park was named Percy Warner Park. The second Warner Park was named for Warner's brother, Edwin, who eventually became the driving force in preserving much of the land acquired following the initial donation. Lea's Summit, a scenic overlook in Percy Warner Park, commemorates the efforts of Colonel Lea.

Warner Parks were developed in the 1930s when President Franklin Roosevelt's New Deal program provided the Works Progress Administration with funds to construct recreational facilities within the new urban park. Many of the WPA projects are still visible. The seven limestone entrances, stone bridges, picnic shelters, and the steeplechase are but a few of the WPA's projects.

Today the area's wooded hills and valleys are surrounded by residential development, so the parks have come to offer a sanctuary within an otherwise busy urban setting. Much of the forest here has been relatively undisturbed for many decades,

and scenic drives throughout both parks are shaded by massive trees. Large American beech trees, an indicator of a climax forest, are commonplace. In Percy Warner Park, a sassafras tree measuring three feet in diameter is Tennessee's largest. White-tailed deer, coyote, red fox, and raccoon all thrive there. More than 300 species of wildflowers and some 180 species of birds have been identified in the park, making this one of the state's outstanding natural areas. The 2,681-acre park was placed on the Tennessee register of natural areas in 1980, a testament to its excellent natural and recreational values.

Horseback riding is popular at Percy Warner Park, where more than fifteen miles of bridle trails have been designated for equestrian use during daylight hours. The trail head is at the equestrian center next to the site of the celebrated Iroquois Steeplechase. The steeplechase was constructed by the WPA and is the only track of its kind built as a New Deal project. The Iroquois Steeplechase is held the second Saturday in May and has been a yearly event since 1946.

Two golf courses are found in the park. The nine-hole Percy Warner Golf Course is next to the main entrance to Percy Warner Park adjacent to

Belle Meade Boulevard. Harpeth Hills Golf Course, an eighteen-hole course, is west of Chickering Road on Old Hickory Boulevard.

Recreational facilities in the area include fields for baseball, soccer, remote-control aircraft, and polo. Other fields scattered throughout the area are open to recreational activities such as Frisbee throwing and other sports. A small fishing lake is just off Highway 100 in Percy Warner Park. There are four main picnic sites—Little Harpeth River, Indian Springs, Deep Well, and Beech Grove—and a number of picnic shelters and tables throughout the area.

The Warner Parks have a system of scenic drives that twist and turn through the hills and hollows of both parks. Many WPA structures are visible along these drives. Several roads in Edwin Warner Park have been closed to vehicle traffic but are open to pedestrians.

More than ten miles of trails are found in Warner Parks. The Deep Well picnic area in Percy Warner Park serves as the trail head for two loop trails, totaling seven miles of moderately difficult hiking trails. The main trail head for Edwin Warner Park begins behind the Warner Park Nature Center. Six trails, most of them loop trails, range from three-tenths of a mile to two and a half miles and provide easy-to-moderate hiking. Several of Edwin Warner's trails are self-guided nature trails. Mountain-bike riding is not allowed on any trail.

The Warner Park Nature Center is the hub of the educational efforts for the area. The office and

Barred Owl

Tennessee's most commonly seen and heard owl is the Barred Owl, often referred to as a hoot owl because of its eight-hoot call that

seems to ask, "Who cooks for you? Who cooks for you all?" When excited or in a group, the birds yelp and scream an almost monkeylike call. Their cries are heard at practically any time of the day or night. Barred Owls are found primarily in wooded areas and are usually seen by hikers during daylight hours. This species is the state's most active daytime (diurnal) owl.

A dark brown, mottled color, dark brown eyes, and the absence of ear tufts distinguish the Barred Owl from the Great Horned Owl, which is a larger bird with yellow eyes and ear tufts. Tennessee's only other owl with dark eyes is the Barn Owl, which is almost completely white in color. Soft, fluffy feathers allow the Barred Owl to fly silently through its woodland habitat in search of rodent prey. These soft feathers give the owl an almost teddy bear–like appearance.

Barred Owls are found throughout the parks of Tennessee, although Percy and Edwin Warner parks and Radnor Lake have particularly large and visible populations that are accustomed to people and often perch unconcerned near curious observers.

library are staffed Monday through Friday, and a natural history museum is open upon request during these days. The museum houses a number of natural history exhibits, among them an egg collection and an aquarium. The building is named for a Vanderbilt University zoologist, Dr. Charles Farrell, who is recognized as one of Nashville's outstanding conservationists. A variety of conservation demonstration activities are in progress at the nature center, including a bird-feeding area, a wildflower and organic garden and compost area, beehives, and a weather station.

The nature center staff conducts numerous programs throughout the year and engages in a variety of research projects. The public is frequently invited to participate in research projects such as bird tagging and exotic plant removal. One project of special note is the bluebird project started by Amelia Laskey in 1936. Mrs. Laskey established a bluebird trail and kept meticulous records of bluebird nesting patterns until her death in 1973. Twenty years later, the bluebird trail and research continue as one of the country's oldest continuously running projects of its kind.

From Nashville, travel south on Hwy. 100 to Old Hickory Blvd. To the north of Old Hickory Blvd. is Percy Warner Park, to the south is Edwin Warner Park. The Warner Park Nature Center is a short distance southeast of this intersection. The park headquarters is on Vaughn Rd., just off Old Hickory Blvd. Other entrances to the parks are from Belle Meade Blvd. and Chickering Rd.

Woodchuck

The woodchuck or groundhog is a common sight along roadsides and the edges of fields throughout the state. Once it has begun its preparation for winter hibernation, it becomes a perpetual-eating machine, dining on almost any kind of vegetation. It is not a particularly welcome guest in agricultural areas because of its healthy appetite for young plants. Sometimes a woodchuck is so fat it seems to flow along the ground when running. This thickset mammal is occasionally mistaken for a beaver because of its broad, fur-covered tail, although a beaver's tail is scaly and furless. The woodchuck weighs approximately twelve pounds when full grown and has reddish gray fur. It is a strong burrowing animal, digging a network of burrows with two or more openings that extend up to thirty feet in length. Woodchucks hibernate from late October to February and usually snooze right through Groundhog Day on February 2.

Warner Park Nature Center
7311 Highway 100
Nashville, TN 37221
(615) 352-6299

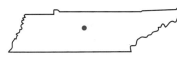

Warner Park Headquarters
50 Vaughn Road
Nashville, TN 37221
(615) 370-8050

March–May	Bluebirds nesting
March	Wildflowers begin blossoming
May	Second Saturday, Iroquois Steeplechase
October 21	Beech and maple trees at height of autumnal colors

Radnor Lake State Natural Area

As a curtain of mist lifts from Radnor Lake in the early morning, the water's surface reflects the nearby Overton Hills and banks lined with sycamore, cottonwood, and willow trees. The quiet of the lake is broken by sounds of largemouth bass foraging for food and Canada Geese announcing their departure. White-tailed deer and their young tentatively step to the water's edge to drink during the solitude of the early hours.

Radnor Lake State Natural Area's pastoral setting conceals the lake's man-made origin. It was created in 1914 when South Nashville's Otter Creek was impounded to provide water for the steam locomotives of the L&N Railroad. Today most of the scars left by this industrial use or by earlier logging and farming enterprises are hidden within the 1,050 acres of one of Tennessee's most popular natural areas.

The uniqueness of Radnor Lake is periodically underlined at times when this small slice of wilderness is threatened. In 1973, a residential community was being planning for the area. The only way to block the development was to purchase the land outright for $3.5 million, and the proponents of Radnor Lake had less than a month to secure the funds. State and federal funding for the project fell a half million dollars short of the price. But the citizens of Nashville and the surrounding area did

what many thought was impossible: in three short weeks they raised the needed funds and preserved the natural environment of the lake, which later that year became Tennessee's first natural area.

Often referred to as Nashville's Walden Pond, Radnor Lake has provided a quiet haven for its visitors. The Walt Criley Visitors Center hosts exhibits and educational programs on the natural and cultural history of the area. Six miles of easy-to-strenuous hiking trails wind around the lake through the surrounding hills. A self-guided nature trail at the west parking area interprets the natural resources of the area.

For an urban natural area, Radnor Lake boasts a remarkable diversity and abundance of wildlife. Shortly after the lake's construction, large numbers of birds began migrating to the area. Approximately 240 species have been identified since the area became popular for wildlife viewing. The spring and fall flights of vireos, warblers, and other songbirds can be easily viewed from the top of the dam and from the Lake Trail. Barred Owls are frequently seen and heard along other trails, and Great Horned Owls are heard at sunset in the Hall Farm area.

Canada Geese are year-round residents, sometimes numbering in the hundreds. When joined by migratory geese in the fall, large numbers can be

Canada Goose

Tennessee's largest and most visible species of waterfowl is the Canada Goose, which can now be seen throughout the state on any substantial lake or river. The Canada Goose is easily identified by its white cheek patch and black neck and head. The wings and back are a grayish brown, and the tail is black with a broad white band. Canada Geese are highly vocal and can often be heard over great distances where large flocks occur.

The Canada Goose engages in very animated courtship and territorial displays. In February and March courtship may be observed as breeding pairs separate from family groups. Nesting begins in April, with the first goslings appearing in late April or early May. Visitors to Tennessee parks should be warned that adult birds are extremely protective of their nests and young birds and will not hesitate to flog intruders with their powerful wings. By early June the flightless molt begins. This molt is an interesting survival strategy that affects most species of waterfowl: all flight feathers are molted at once, leaving all adult birds flightless at the same time. The regrowth of flight feathers in the adult birds coincides with the fledging of young goslings. By early July, the entire flock begins to fly short flights to feeding areas in preparation for the fall migration.

Migrating flocks from the north begin to arrive in late October and early November. These nonresident migrating geese oftentimes mix with resident flocks to form very large flocks. Refuges such as Reelfoot Lake routinely have thousands of geese that can be viewed as they travel to and from feeding areas during the winter months.

seen cartwheeling downward to overnight resting spots as darkness falls. Since the area closes at sunset, visitors must secure permission from the visitors center to stay late to observe this spectacle. From October through April, as many as twenty-six other species of waterfowl, such as Wood Ducks, Canvasbacks, and Mallards, can be seen on the large slough and eighty-five-acre lake. The Wood Duck became the symbol of Radnor Lake during a citizen drive to save the area. It is the only duck species to nest regularly at Radnor and may be seen year-round.

In addition to encountering deer on the trails, hikers often come across muskrats patrolling the lake. The more secretive mink and bobcats are occasionally glimpsed in the underbrush, and the excited yelps and howls of resident coyotes can be heard as a resident family claims ownership of the night.

In the spring, spectacular displays of wildflowers beckon hikers to the trails across the ridges and along the lake. Trillium, dwarf larkspur, trout lily, Dutchman's breeches, spring beauties, and dozens of other wildflowers are especially prominent on the south side of the lake. In the fall, wildflowers offer a vivid show of purples and yellows throughout the fields, especially around the Hall Farm. During spring and summer, millions of tiny lime-green duckweed plants cover the surface of the slough and lake, and white water crowfoot scatter their blossoms like small cotton balls across the water's surface.

For a rewarding view of downtown Nashville framed through an opening in the chestnut-oak forest, hikers climb to the summit of the strenuous Ganier Ridge Trail, one and a half miles long. This view and other signs of the natural area's urban location provide a constant reminder of Radnor Lake's significant role in the natural landscape of Tennessee.

From Interstate 65 south of Nashville, take the Harding Place exit west to Franklin Road. Take Franklin Road south, less than two miles, to the second traffic light. Otter Creek Road, which runs through the middle of the natural area, will be to the right; it provides access to the parking lots on the east and west ends of the area and to the visitors center at the west parking lot.

Bobcat

One of Tennessee's least-often-seen large animals, the bobcat is the state's only surviving native cat. An extremely reclusive animal with mottled tan fur that allows it to blend into its surroundings, the bobcat can be found throughout the state. While most parks probably have bobcats, very few can prove it; even the tracks of this mammal are hard to find. The bobcat is roughly the size of a small dog and weighs up to fifty pounds. As its name implies, it has a "bobbed" or short tail. The bobcat is a true carnivore, primarily eating small mammals and birds. It has been known, however, to kill small deer. The animal's hunting style is similar to that of other cats. It crouches low to the ground and waits for the right moment to pounce. The bobcat is primarily a nocturnal hunter, but when encountered during daylight hours in forested areas, it is usually stalking birds. One of the best ways to recognize a bobcat is by its call, which has been described as similar to the wail of a woman or a baby.

Radnor Lake State Natural Area
1160 Otter Creek Road
Nashville, TN 37220
Office phone: (615) 373-3467
For program information and reservations: (615) 377-1281

February	Harbingers-of-spring begin to blossom
April	Nature hikes and canoe floats offered
April-May	Spring warbler flights along the Lake Trail and across the top of the spillway
September-October	Fall warbler flights at their peak
October	Wildflower, nature hikes, and canoe floats available
November	Migrating flocks of Canvasback, Bufflehead, and other winter waterfowl begin to arrive

Natchez Trace Parkway

Winding through the forests between Natchez, Mississippi, and Nashville, Tennessee, a series of Native American and wildlife trails were joined nearly two hundred years ago to form what is now called the Natchez Trace Parkway. *Natchez* was the city of origin, and *trace* comes from the French word for *trail*.

During its heyday, the Trace was heavily used as a boatman's trail. The Cumberland, Ohio, and Tennessee rivers that connected to the Mississippi provided easy access to southern ports, but overland routes, including the Natchez Trace, were more difficult, and transporting large cargo was practically impossible. Thus the Natchez Trace was more popular as a return route for boatmen who had shipped their products south by boat or raft. Returning upstream was not an option, since steam-powered paddle wheelers had yet to be developed.

The overland route was celebrated for its difficulties and dangers. A sign at the sunken Trace just north of the Alabama-Tennessee state line perhaps describes the route best: "This early road-building venture produced a snake-infested, mosquito-beset, robber-haunted, Indian-pestered forest path. Lamented by the pious, cussed by the impious, it tried everyone's strength and patience."

The four-hundred-mile Natchez Trace Parkway is managed by the National Park Service. In Ten-

nessee the parkway measures approximately eighty-eight miles. A sign with a mounted horseman surrounded by a circle within an arrowhead is the emblem of the parkway. Wildlife such as white-tailed deer and Red-tailed Hawks are common along the parkway, and there are numerous scenic views of the surrounding countryside. Travelers on the Natchez Trace are encouraged to stop frequently and enjoy the many natural and cultural features. The smooth, winding roadway is a picturesque drive, devoid of the rushing traffic and transport trucks of the interstate. The parkway, however, is more than just a road; it is also a window to an almost forgotten part of the history of Middle Tennessee.

No fewer than twenty-five historic and natural features and support facilities are dotted along the Tennessee portion of the Natchez Trace Parkway. Garrison Creek, at milepost 427.6, offers twenty-five miles of horseback-riding trails, one of four such trails along the parkway. The creek was named for the army garrison that was stationed there during the time of the "government road" or Natchez Trace development.

Jackson Falls (milepost 404.7), named for Andrew Jackson, is a wet-weather falls that drains into the Duck River. A short nine-hundred-foot trail leads to the foot of the falls and the clear-water pool at its base. Overlooks are scattered

along the Trace where the Highland Rim offers the highest elevations and some of the most striking views of the surrounding hill country. Views of the Duck River, Tennessee's largest remaining unimpounded river system, are frequent along this section of the parkway. The Old Trace is marked with horizontal arrowhead-shaped signs where it crisscrosses the parkway.

Several stops along the Trace mark the sites of "stands," where travelers once stopped for shelter and supplies. One such stand was known as She Boss Place. It was run by a widow who had married a Native American who spoke little English. His standard response to any traveler's query was, "She boss," meaning the traveler should ask the wife and avoiding the language barrier.

Old Trace Drive is a narrow, northbound, one-lane road that winds along the original Trace. It provides visitors no fewer than three overlooks with a commanding view of the oak forest in this section. The Napier Mine (milepost 381.8) offers a glimpse of an old open-pit iron mine.

Just south of the Swan Valley overlook is the Fall Hollow Waterfall, one of the most scenic stops in the Tennessee section of the Natchez Trace. Here two waterfall systems drop off the Highland Rim to empty into Big Swan Creek. A short trail, less than a half-mile long, leads past a thirty-foot cascade that ends in a twenty-foot vertical drop into a limestone bowl and clear-water pool. A short distance farther along the trail another small stream plunges into a breathtaking, multilevel, cascading waterfall. The trail winds around both waterfalls and ends at the base of the limestone bowl. Wildflowers in this area are common, with columbine, foamflower, and hepatica being particularly noticeable.

West of the Trace, at milepost 382.8, is Metal Ford. Named for the hard, flat, metal-like rock bottom of the Buffalo River, this part of the river was a preferred ford for travelers crossing the river. McClish's Stand was across the river, reached today by a short interpretive hiking trail that winds along

the river. An old ironworks is barely visible, with only the ancient mill race and small amounts of slag remaining. A twenty-foot limestone bluff line shelters the valley below. A short hiking trail along the top of the bluff affords a view of the entire Metal Ford complex. Beech trees, laurel, foamflower, and maidenhair fern grace the surrounding woodlands.

At milepost 385.9, two miles east of Hohenwald, is the Meriwether Lewis Site. Lewis, once a personal secretary to Thomas Jefferson and later famous for his role in the Lewis and Clark Expedition, met an untimely death in October 1809 at the age of thirty-five at the Grinder House, which stood on this site. His death from a gunshot wound was either suicide or murder. Recent tests to try to determine the cause of his death have been inconclusive. Lewis's grave is marked with a stone monument. The district ranger office contains exhibits about the site. Picnic areas and a thirty-two-site campground without hookups are also available.

North of Collinwood, at milepost 363 is the Sweetwater Branch Nature Trail. This short, twenty-minute loop trail winds through the creek bottoms surrounding Sweetwater Branch. It is an easy walk on a level trail that provides a close look at one of the many streams found along the route. Self-guided trail signs interpret many of the natural and geological features along the trail. More than a hundred species of wildflowers grow here. Wood Duck and other wildlife can be seen along the stream-side trail. Just north of the trail beavers have dammed a section of Sweetwater Branch to form a series of ponds that can be seen directly west of the Trace, where the stream passes near the roadway.

At several locations visitors can comprehend the hardships endured by long-ago travelers. At milepost 403.7, for example, a two-thousand-foot section of the Old Trace provides a short walk where wagons and ox carts wore down the roadbed several feet below the level of the surrounding woodlands.

Sunken Trace, at milepost 350.5, shows where muddy conditions that mired ox carts caused shifting of the Trace to no less than three routes over a short stretch.

From Nashville, take Hwy. 96 west from Franklin to the current terminus of the parkway. The planned final terminus, expected to be completed in 1995, will be at Hwy. 100, approximately ten miles south of Nashville near Pasquo. Approximately ten other access ramps along the parkway provide access to communities adjacent to the Trace. These communities offer the only food and gas service along the Tennessee section of the parkway. Maps of the Natchez Trace Parkway available along the route indicate the stops and locations of many of these communities. The trip along the Tennessee section of the parkway provides an educational one-day outing for Middle Tennesseans.

Lizards

Lizards are the most commonly encountered reptiles in Tennessee, fond of sunning themselves along fence rows and around houses. Most lizards are small, usually less than twelve inches long, except for the glass lizard, which can reach three or more feet in length. Lizards, which are scaly reptiles, are distinguished from snakes by the presence of visible eardrums, movable eyelids, four legs, and clawed toes. The glass lizard is an exception and has no legs. Lizards can be distinguished from salamanders, which have a similar body form but lack scales and have clawless toes.

Many lizards have interesting defense mechanisms. Skinks, for

example, have fragile tails that break off when they're caught, leaving the predator with a wiggling reminder of what was once a whole lizard. This fragile section of its tail is frequently very colorful, thus attracting predators to the wrong end of the lizard. The skink will regenerate its tail, although it will usually be shorter and colored differently. Fence lizards are commonly heard before they are seen when their nails grasp a tree or fence. Their cryptic colorations so successfully match the color of the bark of deciduous trees that it can be difficult to spot them unless they move. The anole, rare but sometimes seen in South Central Tennessee, is capable of adjusting its color from pale green to brown or gray to match its immediate surroundings.

The preferred habitat of most lizards is moist and humid woodland, although they are also found around dry, rocky outcroppings.

Natchez Trace Parkway
Rural Route 1, NT 143
Tupelo, MS 38801
(601) 842-1572

February-March	Jackson Falls at its height because of late winter rains
April-May	Columbine and foamflower blossoming around Fall Hollow Falls; Wild Turkey nest
June	Young white-tailed deer and Wild Turkey highly visible
Late September	Red-tailed Hawks migrating along the roadway
October 15	Fall colors at their peak

Land Between the Lakes

Land Between the Lakes is a Tennessee Valley Authority development project. Surrounded on three sides by the impounded waters of Lake Barkley and Kentucky Lake, this area boasts more than three hundred miles of shoreline and 170,000 acres of fields and forests in western Kentucky and Tennessee, making it one of the Southeast's leading wildlife and outdoor recreation areas. The oak-hickory forests here are home to many species of wildlife, and Bald Eagles and buffalo are seen regularly year-round at certain locations throughout the area.

The Land Between the Lakes was also known as the land between the rivers, the Cumberland and the Tennessee. The relative isolation this provided the region allowed the Scotch-Irish settlers to test time-honored family whiskey recipes. Golden Pond, Kentucky, came to be the moonshine capital of the world during the Prohibition years of the 1920s.

Land Between the Lakes was named the world's three hundredth international biosphere reserve in March 1991 as part of the effort of the United Nations' Educational, Scientific, and Cultural Organization's (UNESCO) to conserve examples of the world's ecosystems. In fact, the primary mission of Land Between the Lakes is to allow visitors to explore the natural and cultural features of the area with the help of developed facilities and structured programs.

Just south of the Tennessee-Kentucky border is The Homeplace—1850, where the rural lifestyle of early settlers is demonstrated at a living-history farm. Most of the buildings have been relocated from nearby sites and reassembled to create a farm typical of the 1850s. The Land Between the Lakes staff wear period costumes while carrying on the daily activities of the early farmers.

The Woodlands Nature Center is at Honker Lake, the centerpiece of environmental education at Land Between the Lakes. Exhibits showcase red wolves, bald and golden eagles, white-tailed and fallow deer, and several other wildlife species. Educational programs are presented to enhance the visitors' understanding of the area, and several day-hike trails provide access to Hematite and Honker lakes.

The Golden Pond complex on the Kentucky side of Land Between the Lakes is the area's main visitors center. Situated at the junction of the Trace, the area's main north-south road, and Highway 68, the visitors center features cultural history exhibits, a gift shop, and a planetarium. The planetarium features an eighty-eight-seat auditorium with a

forty-foot screen; an observatory is also open at specified times and dates.

Lake Barkley and Kentucky Lake provide a variety of recreational opportunities. The large impoundments and several smaller lakes within the area offer some of the best sport fishing in the region. Access to the large lakes is provided to boaters by ten boat-launching ramps. Picnic areas can be found along most of the developed facilities and near the launch ramps. Hunting is permitted throughout much of the area.

Camping is another popular activity at Land Between the Lakes. The campgrounds within the area—Energy Lake, Piney, and Hillman Ferry—provide electrical and water hookups at nearly six hundred campsites. Hillman Ferry and Piney campgrounds are near Kentucky Lake; Energy Lake campground is a small thirty-five-site campground on the Lake Barkley side of the area. Rushing Creek campground is opened seasonally; drinking water and showers are available. There are ten lake-access areas that provide limited numbers of less-developed campsites.

The trail system at Land Between the Lakes is designed to accommodate a wide spectrum of trail users. Mountain-bike trails are open at Energy Lake and Jenny Ridge. The numbered and backwoods roads are also open to biking. At Wranglers Campground, there are approximately thirty-five miles of equestrian trails. The Turkey Bay off-highway vehicle area provides miles of trails for off-road enthusiasts, and hiking trails are scattered throughout the area. The Honker and Hematite trails for day-use hiking allow many opportunities to glimpse the area's wildlife. Of the nearly one hundred miles of backpacking trails, the sixty-five-mile North-South Trail is the longest. Primitive back-country camping is allowed in most areas of Land Between the Lakes unless otherwise posted.

Take U.S. Hwy. 79 to Dover, Tennessee. Two entrances are situated just west of Dover, at the Trace, and at Fort Henry Road, just east of Kentucky Lake. Land Between the Lakes is east of Paris, Tennessee, and west of Clarksville, Tennessee.

Green Heron

Although somewhat solitary in nature, the Green Heron is one of Tennessee's most common herons. Its name, however, is not particularly accurate, since this small crow-sized bird is more of a grayish green or blue. Its neck, which is shorter than most herons, is reddish brown with vertical white striping on the chest. The Green Heron is most commonly seen on the edge of a lake, crouched motionless on a log or low tree branch waiting for small fish to surface. Most parks with bodies of water have at least a few scattered Green Herons. Their nesting behavior differs from most other herons, as they prefer to nest alone rather than in colonies.

One of the more interesting behavioral traits in this species is its fishing strategy. It drops small bits of vegetation onto the water so it can catch small fish as they surface to investigate.

Raccoon

The masked bandit of the forest is the subject of countless stories about its legendary curiosity. Tennessee's raccoons are highly adaptable and are found throughout the state in both urban and rural settings. Perhaps because of huge amounts of trash or the handouts of well-intentioned people, raccoons seem to thrive in metropolitan settings. Residents of some cities and suburbs have as many as fifteen or more raccoons to visit their homes each evening for an easy meal. People, of course, enjoy watching the raccoons because they are one of nature's most engaging,

even entertaining, animal species. Nonetheless, it should be noted that while feeding wildlife can be very interesting, it can compromise their wildness and diminish their natural wariness. As a result, they can become easy targets for larger predators. Furthermore, unnaturally high population levels of cer-

tain species created by artificial food sources can have devastating effects in the case of disease. The message here is that it is neither possible nor wise to try to take the "wild" out of wildlife.

The black mask, dark brown eyes, humanlike hands, and ringed tail make this animal a favorite of nature lovers. The raccoon is an excellent climber and swimmer, seen in the wild primarily at night foraging near water. It is an omnivorous animal, eating grains, fruits, eggs, and other animals. The characteristic "washing" of food by raccoons is likely a foraging behavior rather than an endeavor to clean the food.

Land Between the Lakes
Golden Pond, KY 42231
(502) 924-5602

January-February	Eagle population at its height; February known for "Eagle Weekends"
March	Wood Ducks begin nesting late in the month
April-May	Good fishing for large-slab crappie with minnows
June-August	The Homeplace—1850 living-history demonstrations
September	Trees marked by white-tailed bucks rubbing summer velvet from their antlers
November	Bald Eagles begin returning to the area

Natchez Trace State Park and Forest

Visitors who travel the main roads through Natchez Trace State Park and Forest near Lexington will notice many green-and-white posts with the names of fire trails that connect to the paved roads. Signs bearing names like Taylor, Derryberry, and Woods honor families that once called this area home. During the early 1900s, farming the fragile, sandy soils held little hope for a better tomorrow. The land was poorly suited for the farming techniques of that time and became severely eroded into gullies. Roosevelt's New Deal relocated families outside the park area and, in many cases, offered the farmers jobs reclaiming and developing the land that once belonged to them.

Originally, Natchez Trace State Park was established during the Great Depression as a demonstration area where unemployed Americans could find jobs with the Civilian Conservation Corps and the Works Progress Administration, undertaking numerous conservation activities to help the area recover. Loblolly pine and black locust were planted extensively to control erosion, and thousands of erosion-control check dams were constructed to slow the growing gullies. Recreation facilities, including picnic areas, cabins, a group camp, and a recreation lodge, were built, and Brown's Creek, Cub Creek, and Maple Creek were all dammed to provide fishing and water recreation.

As the nation recovered from the Great Depression, so too has the land. Today, tall stands of loblolly pine line the roads of the Natchez Trace parkland. The check dams that once controlled the erosion have all but vanished, and large patches of kudzu spread where the plant was introduced to control erosion. During the summer months the kudzu gives these areas an almost rainforest-like appearance. Some of the original cabins and buildings are still in use. Active forest and wildlife management are evident in the numerous wildlife food plots scattered throughout the area. White-tailed deer, red and gray fox, and coyotes are frequently seen from the roadside.

Natchez Trace State Park received its name from the overland route connecting Nashville and Natchez, Mississippi. A western variant of the famous Natchez Trace lies alongside and often directly beneath the main road passing through the park. The forty-five-thousand-acre plot is now managed for multiple use by three separate agencies: Tennessee Division of Forestry, Tennessee State Parks, and Tennessee Wildlife Resources Agency.

This multiple-use management provides many opportunities for outdoor recreation. More than

Great Blue Heron

The Great Blue Heron is North America's tallest and largest heron. Found alongside bodies of water throughout Tennessee, it is easily identified by its tall, long-legged form (up to four feet in height), and its slate gray coloring. Like many herons, the great blue sports feathery plumes on its chest and head. These birds are most often seen in shallow water in search of food. Great blues can be distinguished from Sandhill Cranes, which migrate through Tennessee, by their flight patterns: Great blues fold their necks in and the cranes extend their necks out. A great blue in flight is distinguished by its call, a hoarse-sounding guttural squawk.

five hundred miles of fire trails crisscross the area, providing trails for horseback and mountain-bike enthusiasts. A wrangler camp on the area's south side can accommodate the camping equestrian. Three campgrounds are also in the area. Bucksnort Campground provides convenient access to Interstate 40, which bisects the area; two other campgrounds at Cub Lake provide access to the swimming area, boat dock, and recreation lodge.

The fifty-mile Red Leaves Trail is a national scenic trail traversing the northern and southern portions of the area. Intermittent primitive campsites have been developed along the trail. Twelve miles of day-use hiking trails provide routes around Cub Lake and through the forests. The Fairview Gullies Trail offers a glimpse of an erosion gully and its reclamation. Formerly it was a hundred feet deep and more than a mile long, one of the worst gullies in the area.

On a dry hilltop in the northern section of Natchez Trace Park stands a grand old pecan tree. Nearly eighteen feet in circumference, it is one of the largest pecan trees in the world. Legend has it that one of Andrew Jackson's men, returning from the battle of New Orleans, gave the original tree to a local girl, Sukey Morris, who later planted its seed. The tree overlooks a developed picnic site that is easily accessible from the main park road.

Four lakes fall within the boundaries of the park and forest. Two of the lakes, Brown's Creek Lake and Maple Creek Lake, are managed for fishing by the Tennessee Wildlife Resources Agency. Both lakes are less than a hundred acres and are quite productive. Brown's Creek Lake, for example, yielded a state-record, four-pound, four-ounce, black crappie in 1985. Cub Lake, the smallest of the lakes, is used primarily for recreational pursuits, such as paddle boating and swimming. Twenty rustic cabins line the shores of Cub Lake.

Comprising seven hundred acres, Pin Oak Lake is the largest and most developed of the four lakes and is the only one where water-skiing is permitted. Two launching ramps provide access to the lake. Twenty-room Pin Oak Lodge on the banks of the lake is a well-kept secret. The smallest of the inns in the Tennessee State Park System, Pin Oak exudes a less-hurried atmosphere than the larger resort developments. A restaurant, tennis courts, and a swimming pool are open to guests of the lodge.

Take Interstate 40 to exit 116 and follow the signs to the part of the park you wish to visit. The park headquarters are three miles south of the interstate.

Red and Gray Fox

Two species of fox are found in Tennessee. Both red and gray foxes are striking animals, approximately the size of small dogs, weighing seven to fifteen pounds. Although foxes are primarily nocturnal hunters, they are occasionally seen during daylight hours. Both foxes are omnivorous by nature, but the gray fox tends to be decidedly more vegetarian. These mammals inhabit forests and fields through-out the state, and most parks have one or both species.

The red fox is a highly adaptable predator that is found throughout North America. Though secretive, it is tolerant of human activities and is often seen in urban and metropolitan surroundings. The red coloring is usually a good field sign; colors in this species, how-ever, can vary widely. A white tip on the tail is a more reliable sign.

The gray fox is a sly and secre-tive predator that appears to be smiling when feeding. The gray fox has semiretractable nails that allow it to engage in limited climbing to escape other predators or to catch prey. It is more secretive than the red fox and much less tolerant of human contact. For this reason, the gray fox is more often seen in rural areas.

Natchez Trace State Park and Forest

March-April	Spring wildflowers blossoming throughout the park, turtles emerging from hibernation seen sunning on logs on the area lakes
June	Large numbers of Whippoorwill seen along the roadside north of I-40
August	Purple blossoms of kudzu fill the air with a grape fragrance
September 1	Hunting season begins for many wildlife—check with the park office before hiking
September 15	Wood Ducks preparing for southern migration
October 1	Fall wildflowers adding splashes of white and orange to the field cover; monarch butterflies migrating through the area

Meeman-Shelby State Park

When you watch the sun set across the Mississippi River from Meeman-Shelby State Park, you are overwhelmed by the sheer magnitude of the "Father of Waters." The swift current is inconspicuous until a barge passes, battling its way upstream. Meeman-Shelby is Tennessee's most visited state park, twelve thousand acres on Chickasaw Bluff just north of Memphis in Shelby County.

The winding roads through the park crisscross hills and valleys beneath tall stands of southern hardwood. Giant tree limbs hover over the roadways, shading the pavement and its travelers. The forest is home to a profusion of wildlife; white-tailed deer and Wild Turkey are commonly seen throughout the area. The Mississippi River and this woodlands together form a memorable natural area.

Meeman-Shelby State Park honors the memory of Edward J. Meeman, an avid conservationist instrumental in the establishment of the Great Smoky Mountains National Park. In 1933 as editor of the *Memphis Press-Scimitar*, he called for the preservation of Shelby forest. He wrote, "The newspaper can accomplish many things. Public support can accomplish many things. But the newspaper with public support can accomplish most anything."

Just like many other Tennessee parks, the project began as a forest demonstration area under the auspices of the Resettlement Administration and the National Park Service. The goal was the eventual leasing or deeding of the area to the state for use as a state park. After the Tennessee State Park System was established in 1937, the administrative responsibility shifted to the state. The transfer of the deed to the Tennessee Department of Conservation in 1944 made Meeman-Shelby, then known as Shelby Forest Park, one of Tennessee's earliest state parks.

Many of the New Deal's Works Progress Administration projects still exist and are central to the popularity of the area, although recent developments have added to the park's attractiveness. In the northwest corner, a boat launch facilitates access to the Mississippi River. A fifty-site campground contains level sites and full hookups. A large stone memorial transported from the Great Smoky Mountains details the conservation efforts of Edward J. Meeman. Near the Chickasaw Bluffs Trail, a camp offers overnight accommodations for large groups. Poplar Tree Lake has six vacation cabins and a boat dock. Fishing on this lake for bass, bluegill, and catfish is rated as outstanding. Other facilities include a recreation lodge, swimming

Frogs and Toads

Frogs and toads are Tennessee's most talkative amphibians. On warm spring evenings the forests come alive with the often deafening songs of spring peepers. More than fifteen species of frogs and toads are found in the state, easily distinguished from other amphibians by their powerful hind limbs, the absence of tails in adults, and a short, round body shape.

True frogs are generally considered to be every animal in this order that is not a toad or a tree frog. The skin of true frogs is smoother, the hind legs are longer and better adapted for leaping, and the hind toes are webbed. A large eardrum is visible in most species. Most frogs are found in or near water. Many times the presence of frogs will go unnoticed until weather conditions stimulate a breeding urge that can cause large numbers of frogs to congregate around the edges of lakes and streams. The bullfrog is one of the largest and most common frogs.

Pickeral frog

Toads usually have a dry, warty skin. Their hind legs are shorter to provide a hopping style of locomotion. Toads are not capable of producing warts on humans; the glands on their backs are designed to deter predators. When a toad feels threatened, these glands secrete an irritant to the mucous membranes around the eyes and elsewhere on its attacker. Most toads have pronounced paratoid glands, large lumps behind the eyes, that make identification easier. Their distinctive egg masses are laid in strings. American and Fowler's toads are often seen on warm summer evenings foraging for insects around sidewalks and roadways.

Tree frogs are a large family of frogs that include the tree, chorus, and cricket frogs, with approximately ten species found in Tennessee. Although they look somewhat like true frogs, the hind toes are not as distinctly webbed and the skin is less smooth. They are primarily tree dwelling with specially adapted toes to facilitate climbing. The cricket frog is the exception to this rule. They do not have toe discs and do not climb. This family of frogs is rarely seen but commonly heard. The chorus frogs are the earliest singers in this family. The mating urge is triggered by the first warm rains of spring. In the Deep South mating may begin in November, hence the name winter frogs.

Gray tree frog

pool, picnic areas with five picnic shelters, a disc or Frisbee golf course, riding stables, and a bike trail.

Within this area more than twenty miles of hiking and equestrian trails wind throughout the forests. The six-mile Chickasaw Bluffs Trail, a state scenic trail, penetrates large stands of bottomland hardwood, primarily beech and oak trees. Since the park is also a wildlife management area, the trails are closed for hunting during certain seasons, notably, fall deer and spring turkey hunts.

From Interstate 240 in Memphis, travel north on North Watkins Street until it joins Locke Cuba Road. Turn left three-quarters of a mile to Bluff Road and right one mile to the park entrance. The route to Meeman-Shelby is well marked from the I-240 exit.

Wild Turkey

The Wild Turkey—Benjamin Franklin's choice for our national symbol—can be seen in Tennessee with increasing regularity. Standing up to four feet tall and weighing up to twenty-five pounds, it is the state's largest bird. From a distance its coloration is a drab brown, but closer inspection finds the bird's coloring to be an iridescent splash of bronze. Its naked head and wattles change from blue to red depending on the bird's mood. Males are distinguished by their

comparatively larger size, spurs on their legs, and a long growth of feathers extending from their chest, called a beard. This beard sometimes grows as long as twelve inches in mature males. Occasionally, a hen will have a beard, but it is generally less than three inches long. Fall is the best season for observing Wild Turkeys in flocks of up to several hundred birds. Wild Turkeys can be seen at Land Between the Lakes, Big South Fork, Cade's Cove in the Great Smoky Mountains, and Meeman-Shelby State Park.

Meeman-Shelby State Park
Route 3
Millington, TN 38053
(901) 876-5201

March	Wildflowers beginning to bloom
May	Migrating Mississippi Kites returning to nest along the river early in the month
June-August	Excellent largemouth bass fishing, especially with top-water plugs
September	Large groups of turkeys beginning to flock together
November	Peak autumnal colors of beech and tulip poplar trees early in the month

Reelfoot Lake

Reelfoot Lake is unsullied by the crowded ways of civilization. From the top of a tall cypress tree a Bald Eagle surveys the lake for an easy meal. In the distance, the raucous honks of a flock of Canada Geese shatter the silence as thousands depart from the refuge en route to nearby fields and feeding areas. Dark-shaded areas are created by the dense foliage of the bald cypress trees, whose knees (or roots) extend through the water's surface. A heavy-bodied cottonmouth suns itself in the hot days of summer.

Containing Tennessee's only natural lake, the nearly thirty-thousand-acre Reelfoot Lake area is a wild and scenic area that was formed when the New Madrid earthquakes of 1811 and 1812 changed the channel of the Mississippi River. The earthquakes were so powerful that diary accounts describe the floodplain soil as rippling in waves and the river flowing backward. The name *Reelfoot* memorializes a Chickasaw chief's son who reeled or staggered because of a club foot.

Perhaps the best feature of Reelfoot Lake is its bird population. Approximately 250 of the more than 300 species of birds in Tennessee can be found there, the most conspicuous being the Bald Eagle. A federally endangered species, the Bald Eagle is a year-round resident of the area. During the winter months, more than a hundred eagles may winter on Reelfoot Lake and the nearby Mississippi River. With fish as their primary food source, the eagles feed freely on the usually ice-free lake. One of the best places from which to view the eagles is the observation deck at the Airpark Inn. Other places where eagles may be seen are along the Blue Bank area and along Highway 22 toward the town of Samburg. The refuge and Kirby Pocket day-use area may also have eagles.

The shallow waters of Reelfoot Lake also attract large numbers of waterfowl. More than a hundred thousand geese and nearly a half million ducks winter in the area. Most of these species are seen in the refuge section of the lake. Mississippi Kites are

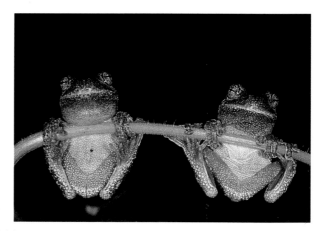

Bald Eagle

The recovery of the Bald Eagle is perhaps the best testament to our ability to preserve and protect an endangered natural resource. Tennessee populations of Bald Eagles have increased through intensive wildlife-management programs. Winter sightings are possible on the state's larger lakes and rivers. Since the eagle's diet is primarily fish, a large percentage of these birds of prey are concentrated in the northwest corner of Tennessee where Reelfoot Lake, Land Between the Lakes, and the nearby confluence of the Ohio and Mississippi rivers provide a steady food source.

The familiar white head and tail of the mature Bald Eagle offer good, if not definitive, field characteristics, since immature eagles lack these features. Adult coloration is rarely complete until the fourth or fifth year. Eagles can usually be distinguished from other native birds of prey by the large size of even young birds. The wingspan can reach up to more than six feet.

also spotted occasionally on the river, and numerous species of gulls and herons can be found around the lake.

The natural area provides habitats for many other wildlife, including river otters, beaver, and white-tailed deer. Thousands of turtles may be seen sunning themselves, and water moccasins and water snakes are often encountered around the lake's edge.

The Reelfoot Lake area is cooperatively managed by the U.S. Fish and Wildlife Service at Reelfoot Wildlife Refuge, the Tennessee Wildlife Resources Agency at Reelfoot Wildlife Management Area, and the Reelfoot Lake State Park. The visitors center features exhibits on the natural and cultural history of the area. Of particular interest is an earthquake simulator that facilitates study of the New Madrid Fault and its impact on the formation of Reelfoot Lake. Aquariums and reptile exhibits display specimens of the wildlife of the lake. A Bald Eagle enclosure houses several nonreleasable eagles for a close-up view of Reelfoot's most popular residents. Educational programs are presented at the visitors center throughout the year. From December through mid-March, eagle tours are offered daily for a small fee, with the hour-and-a-half tour being led by an area naturalist.

Facilities at Reelfoot Lake include picnic areas and a seventy-five-site campground. The Airpark

Inn at the north end of the area has a restaurant and twenty cabins that extend over the lake. A deck leading past the cabins terminates at the observation area, one of the best locations from which to view Bald Eagles roosting and foraging. An all-weather airstrip, thirty-five hundred feet long, is adjacent to the inn.

Reelfoot Lake has some of the best freshwater fishing in the entire Southeast. The lake's uniformly shallow depth and the cover generated by the cypress trees provide an ideal habitat for crappies and bluegill, the lake's most popular species (the area is celebrated for its very large bluegill). Private boats may be launched on the lake, and some rental boats are available from private vendors.

From Dyersburg take Hwy. 78 to Tiptonville. To reach the Airpark Inn, continue on Hwy. 78 north of Tiptonville approximately eight miles to Airpark Road; the inn is at the end of the road. To reach the visitors center and the southeast shores of the lake, take Hwy. 21/22 east from Tiptonville.

Reelfoot Lake State Park
Route 1
Tiptonville, TN 38079
(901) 253-7756

December-March	Eagle tours offered, with peak viewing times in January and February
March-April	Bald Eagles departing for northern nesting areas
March-May	Excellent crappie fishing around cypress trees and bushes
May-October	Summer boat cruises and programs
June-September	Summer wildflowers in bloom, particularly lotus and lily pads
November	Bald Eagles and waterfowl beginning to return to the area

Plant Life of Tennessee Parks

Common name	Scientific name	Color corolla	Woody or Herb	Height	Habitat	Native Exotic	Common, Uncommon, or Rare	E	C	W	In bloom
Yellow trillium	Trillium luteum	yellow	H	8"	deciduous forests	N	U	✓	✓		Apr-May
Sessile trillium	Trillium sessile	rust	H	8"	deciduous forests	N	U		✓		Mar-Apr
Jack-in-the-pulpit	Arisaema atrorubens	green	H	8-12"	deciduous forests	N	U	✓	✓	✓	Mar-Apr
Duckweed	Lemna spp.	green	H	1/4"	aquatic	N	C	✓	✓	✓	Mar-Nov
Solomon's seal	Polygonatum biflorum	white	H	2-3'	deciduous forests	N	C	✓	✓	✓	Apr-May
Trout lily	Erythronium americanum	yellow	H	6"	deciduous forests	N	C	✓	✓		Mar-May
Dwarf crested iris	Iris cristata	purple	H	4-8"	deciduous forests	N	U	✓	✓		Apr-May
Pink lady slipper	Cypriedium acaule	pink	H	8-12"	pine forests	N	U	✓	✓	✓	Apr-July
Pokeweed	Phytolacca americana	white	H	6'	disturbed land	N	C	✓	✓	✓	May-Nov
Eastern columbine	Aquilegia canadensis	red	H	12-18"	Limestone outcrops	N	U	✓	✓		Mar-May
Dwarf larkspur	Delphinium tricorne	purple	H	12-18"	deciduous forests	N	C	✓	✓		Mar-May
Hepatica	Hepatica americana	white	H	4-6"	deciduous forests	N	C	✓	✓	✓	Feb-Apr
Mayapple	Podophyllum peltatum	white	H	12-24"	deciduous forests	N	C	✓	✓	✓	Apr-May
Bloodroot	Sanquinaria canadensis	white	H	4-8"	deciduous forests	N	C	✓	✓	✓	Mar-Apr
Spring beauty	Claytonia virginica	white	H	2-4"	deciduous forests	N	C	✓	✓	✓	Mar-Apr
Dutchman's breeches	Dicentra cucullaria	white	H	6-8"	deciduous forests	N	C	✓	✓		Mar-Apr
Indian strawberry	Duchesnia indica	yellow	H	2-4"	disturbed soils	E	C	✓	✓	✓	Feb-Oct
Wild geranium	Geranium maculatum	pink	H	12-24"	deciduous forests	N	C	✓	✓		Apr-June
Poison ivy	Rhus radicans	white	W	vine	open areas	N	C	✓	✓	✓	Apr-May
Virginia creeper	Partenocissus quinquefoli	white	W	vine	open areas	N	C	✓	✓	✓	May-July
Heart a'bustin	Euonymus americanus	white	W	3-6'	deciduous forests	N	C	✓	✓		May-June
Pale jewelweed	Impatiens pallida	yellow	H	2-6'	moist areas	N	C	✓	✓	✓	May-July
Passion flower	Passiflora incarnata	purple	H	vine	fields	N	C		✓		May-July
Prickly pear cactus	Opuntia humifusa	yellow	H	6-12"	dry rocky areas	N	C	✓	✓	✓	May-June
Ginseng	Panax quinquefolium	white	H	8-20"	deciduous forests	N	R	✓	✓	✓	May-June

Common name	Scientific name	Color corolla	Woody or Herb	Height	Habitat	Native Exotic	Common, Uncommon, or Rare	Range in TN E C W	In bloom
Queen Anne's lace	*Daucus carota*	white	H	1-4'	fields	E	C	✓ ✓ ✓	May-Sept
Rhododendron	*Rhododendron spp.*	pink	W	4-6'	mountain tops	N	C	✓ ✓	Apr-July
Mountain laurel	*Kalmia latifolia*	white	W	2-4'	mountain tops	N	C	✓ ✓	Apr-June
Butterfly weed	*Ascelpia tuberosa*	orange	H	18-36"	fields	N	C	✓ ✓ ✓	May-Aug
Phlox	*Phlox carolina*	pink	H	12-36"	deciduous forests	N	C	✓ ✓ ✓	May-July
Phacelia	*Phacelia bipinnatifida*	purple	H	12-24"	deciduous forests	N	C	✓ ✓ ✓	Apr-May
Lyre leaved sage	*Salvia lyrata*	purple	H	12-18"	disturbed soils	N	C	✓ ✓ ✓	Apr-May
Horse nettle	*Solanum carolinense*	purple	H	12-24"	disturbed soils	N	C	✓ ✓ ✓	May-July
Penstemon	*Penstemon canescens*	purple	H	12-24"	fields	N	U	✓ ✓ ✓	Apr-May
Trumpet creeper	*Campsis radicans*	orange	W	vine	fields	N	U	✓ ✓ ✓	Mar-Apr
Cross vine	*Anisostichus capreolata*	orange	W	vine	deciduous forests	N	U	✓ ✓ ✓	Mar-Apr
Coral honeysuckle	*Lonicera sempervirens*	orange	W	vine	deciduous forests	N	C	✓ ✓	Mar-Nov
Elderberry	*Sambucus canadensis*	white	W	3-10'	fields	N	C	✓ ✓ ✓	Apr-May
Cardinal flower	*Lobelia cardinalis*	red	H	24"	moist areas	N	C	✓ ✓	Mar-May
Bellflower	*Campanula americana*	blue	H	2-6'	deciduous forests	N	C	✓ ✓	Apr-May
Ironweed	*Veronia noveboracensis*	purple	H	3-6'	fields	N	C	✓ ✓ ✓	Apr-July
Joe-pye-weed	*Eupatorium fistulosum*	white	H	3-7'	marshes and fields	N	C	✓ ✓	May-Nov
White snakeroot	*Eupatorium rugosum*	white	H	1-4'	deciduous forests	N	C	✓ ✓	Mar-May
Rabbit tobacco	*Gnaphalium obtsifolium*	white	H	1-4'	fields	N	C	✓ ✓ ✓	Mar-May
Frostweed aster	*Aster pilosus*	white	H	1-4'	fields	N	C	✓ ✓ ✓	Feb-Apr
Goldenrod	*Solidago spp.*	yellow	H	2-6'	fields	N	C	✓ ✓ ✓	Apr-May
Black-eyed Susan	*Rudbeckia hirta*	yellow	H	1-3'	fields	N	C	✓ ✓ ✓	Mar-Apr
Yarrow	*Achillea millefolium*	white	H	1-2'	fields	E	C	✓ ✓ ✓	Mar-Apr
Ox-eyed daisy	*Chrysanthemum leucanthemum*	white	H	1-2'	fields	E	C	✓ ✓ ✓	Mar-Apr
Harbinger of spring	*Erigenia bulbosa*	white	H	1-2'	deciduous forests	N	C	✓ ✓ ✓	Feb-Oct

The Other Parks of Tennessee

This tour of Tennessee parks has focused on several of the best and some little-known city, state, and national parks as an introduction to the natural beauty that has been preserved for all Tennesseans. To that end, the state park system was designed to afford every Tennessean an opportunity to enjoy these natural wonders by establishing parks within an hour's drive from any point in the state. This book would be woefully incomplete if it did not offer some information on and directions to the forty state parks and natural areas overseen by the Tennessee State Park System but not described in the preceding text. A map of these parks appears at the end of this section on page 128.

Big Cypress Tree State Natural Area

Kimery Road
Greenfield, TN 38230
(901) 235-2700
Off U.S. Hwy. 45E—This 330-acre natural area lies in the floodplain of the Middle Fork of the Obion River in West Tennessee. It consists of bottomland hardwood forests, including species like bald cypress, tupelo, beaver, and fox squirrel. Contact the area manager for additional information and to arrange tours.

Big Hill Pond State Park

Route 1, Box 150 C
Pocahontas, TN 38061
(901) 645-7967
On State Hwy. 57, located on the junction of the Tuscumbia and Hatchie State Scenic River, the 4,218-acre park provides the visitor with opportunities to understand nature and man's interaction with it. Campsites, backpacking trails, picnic sites, and a visitors center are located within the area. The park includes McNatt Fishing Lake and a cypress-lined pond created during levee construction for the Memphis Charleston Railroad. A boardwalk trail leads into the scenic wetland solitude. The staff provides interpretive and educational activities.

Big Ridge State Park

1015 Big Ridge Road
Maynardville, TN 37807
(615) 992-5523
East of I-75 on State Hwy. 61. The park was developed by TVA and the Civilian Conservation Corps as a demonstration park in the 1930s. This rugged, heavily wooded park includes 3,642 acres overlooking Norris Reservoir. Facilities include a visitors center with nature exhibits, cabins, a group camp, and individual campsites. Its placid lake offers a beach for swimming. Fishing, boating, picnicking, hiking trails, and play areas are also available.

Bledsoe Creek State Park

400 Zieglers Fort Road
Gallatin, TN 37066
(615) 452-3706
Off State Hwy. 25, this 164-acre park is situated on the Bledsoe Creek embayment of the U.S. Corps of Engineers Old Hickory Reservoir near the old 1780s settlement of Cairo in Sumner County. The park provides campsites, all with tables, grills, and electrical hookups. Restrooms with showers and lavatories are conveniently located. Old Hickory Lake provides good boating, skiing, and fishing. Other facilities include two boat-launching ramps and six miles of hiking trail. The historic sites of Wynnewood, Cragfont, Rock Castle, and Fort Bledsoe are nearby.

Booker T. Washington State Park

5801 Champion Road
Chattanooga, TN 37416
(615) 894-4955
Off State Hwy. 58 north of Chattanooga. The park was named for the famous educator Booker Taliaferro Washington. This 353-acre park on the shores of TVA's Chickamauga Reservoir provides a beautiful setting for boating and fishing enthusiasts. Facilities include a swimming pool, picnic areas, and a group camp (no individual campsites). The year-round group lodge, equipped with

complete kitchen facilities, accommodates forty people. There are also a concession building, a boat-launching ramp, spacious fields, and nature trails for hiking. Nearby is Falling Water Falls on Signal Mountain.

Burgess Falls State Natural Area

4000 Burgess Falls Drive
Sparta, TN 38583-8456
(615) 432-5312
Just off State Route 135. The gateway to the Upper Cumberlands, 155-acre Burgess Falls State Natural Area is eight miles south of Interstate 40 near Cookeville. A streamside nature trail winds through lush woodlands, descending below scenic limestone cliffs to the still waters of Center Hill Lake. Falling Water River offers beautiful cascades, the remnants of historic waterworks, and the plunging Burgess Falls. Picnic facilities are available.

Cedars of Lebanon State Park

328 Cedar Forest Road
Lebanon, TN 37087
(615) 443-2769
South of I-40, on U.S. Hwy. 231. Cedars of Lebanon State Park and Forest was named for the Cedars of Lebanon that once existed in the land of King Solomon. Not actually a cedar tree, these eastern junipers were so valuable for pencils, crossties, and cedar oil that the area was cut out by the turn of the century and replanted by the Civilian Conservation Corps in the 1930s. More than twenty native wildflowers can be seen in the cedar glades during the annual wildflower tours in April.

Chickasaw State Park

20 Cabin Lane
Henderson, TN 38340
(901) 989-5141
On U.S. Hwy. 100. This 14,400-acre park and forest was once part of a vast area belonging to the Chickasaw Nation prior to the Jackson Purchase of 1818. Numerous miles of fire roads and trails wind through these scenic timberlands. Nestled among the tall pines on Lake Placid are cabins and the park restaurant. The park includes swimming, boating, fishing, a wrangler camp, a recreation lodge, campground, and hiking trails.

Cove Lake State Park

Route 2, Box 108
Caryville, TN 37714
(615) 562-8355
Off I-75 on U.S. Hwy. 25W. Cove Lake's 673 acres are situated in a beautiful mountain valley setting on the eastern edge of the Cumberland Mountains. There are scenic nature trails and bike trails leading through the open grasslands and woodlands. In the winter, several hundred Canada Geese make this lakeshore their feeding ground. Nearby is the Devil's Race Track whose steep pinnacle rock affords a panoramic view.

Davy Crockett Birthplace State Park

1245 Davy Crockett Park Road
Limestone, TN 37681
(615) 257-2167
Off U.S. Hwy. 11E. This 66-acre historic park just upsteam from the falls of the scenic Nolichucky River is maintained as a memorial to Davy Crockett. Born here 17 August 1786, he moved west with the frontier and was known for his hunting skills, tall tales, and courageous volunteer spirit. This area includes a limestone marker and cabin on the spot where Crockett was born and visitors center exhibits. Nearby is the Cherokee National Forest and his father's "Crockett Tavern" in Morristown.

David Crockett State Park

1440 West Gaines, P.O. Box 398
Lawrenceburg, TN 38464
(615) 762-9408
On U.S. Hwy. 64. Davy Crockett moved his family to the head of Shoal Creek near Lawrenceburg in September 1817. He was elected to the state legislature in 1821 and established a water-powered industrial complex with a powder mill, grist mill, and distillery. The following summer floods washed it all away. The 1,100-acre park has an interpretive center, staffed during the summer months, with exhibits depicting Crockett's life here and a water-powered grist mill. Outdoor dramas are presented in the amphitheater during the summer.

Dunbar Cave State Natural Area

401 Old Dunbar Cave Road
Clarksville, TN 37043
(615) 648-5526
South of U.S. 79. This 110-acre site is honeycombed by caves and sinkholes, the most prominent of which is Dunbar Cave. Excavations revealed that this cave has been occupied by man for thousands of years, drawn by its constant stream flow and natural air conditioning. In the roomy mouth of the cave, square dances, radio shows, and big band era concerts were once held.

Its most famous owner was the great country music star Roy Acuff who had many Grand Ole Opry stars perform here. The cave's legends are numerous. Fishing is permitted in a small scenic lake near the cave entrance. Environmental education programs include cave hikes. These programs are presented throughout the year. Cave hikes for the general public are offered; it is advisable to call for tour schedules.

Edgar Evins State Park

Silver Point, TN 38582
(615) 858-2446
South of I-40 on State Hwy. 96. This 6,280-acre park is located north of Smithville on the steep forested hillsides and clear-water coves of the U.S. Corps of Engineers Center Hill Reservoir. Set in the deep, dissected hills of the Caney Fork River Valley the park attracts boaters, fishermen, and other water sports enthusiasts. A popular fall cruise extends fifty miles upstream to Rock Island State Park.

Fort Loudoun State Historic Park

338 Fort Loudoun Road
Vonore, TN 37885-9756
(615) 884-6217
Off U.S. 411. This 1200-acre site is the location of one of the earliest British fortifications on the western frontier, built in 1756. Nearby were the principal towns of the Cherokee Nation, including Tenase, namesake of the state, and Tuskegee, birthplace of the genius Sequoyah, commemorated by the Cherokee Nation's Museum. Today the fort and the 1794 Tellico Blockhouse overlook TVA's Tellico Reservoir and the Appalachian Mountains. An interpretive center offers information and

artifacts on the area's history that were excavated prior to the fort's reconstruction.

Fort Pillow State Historic Park

Route 2, Box 109 A
Henning, TN 38041
(901) 738-5581
Off U.S. Hwy. 51 and west on State Hwy. 87. The 1,646-acre Fort Pillow, located in Lauderdale County on the Chickasaw Bluffs overlooking the Mississippi River, is rich in both historic and archaeological significance. In 1861, the Confederate Army build extensive fortifications here and named the site for General Gideon J. Pillow of Maury County. Because of its strategic location, the fort was overwhelmed by the Union Army, who controlled it during most of the war. Remains of the earthworks are well preserved. Scenic Cold Creek flows into a bottomland hardwood slough providing a rich wildlife observation area. Nearby are the Hatchie State Scenic River and Chickasaw Wildlife Refuge.

Harpeth Scenic River and Narrows Historic Area

Kingston Springs, TN 37082
(615) 797-9052
Off U.S. Hwy. 70, the Harpeth Scenic River Complex in Davidson County includes the canoe accesses at the U.S. Hwy. 100 Bridge, the 1862 Newsom's Mill ruins, and at the McCrory Lane Bridge at Hidden Lake. Downstream, the Narrows of the Harpeth provides an upstream and downsteam access, the Bell's Bend five-mile float and a unique one-fourth-mile portage. A one-hundred-yard tunnel, hand cut through solid rock, was one of the great engineering feats of the time

and is today an industrial landmark on the National Register of Historic Places. Montgomery Bell, an early iron industrialist, was so proud of his steel mill that he lived within sound of his waterfall and is buried across the river. A mile upstream, Mound Bottom preserves an ancient Indian ceremonial center. Group tours, hiking, and other activities are available.

Harrison Bay State Park

8411 Harrison Bay Road
Harrison, TN 37341
(615) 344-6214
Off State Hwy. 58. The thirty-nine miles of Chickamauga Reservoir shoreline make this 1,199-acre park a water recreation delight. It has one of the most complete marina facilities available on any of the TVA lakes. Wildlife viewing is abundant on Chickamauga Reservoir, with the Savannah Bay mudflats, Booker T. Washington State Park, and the North Chickamauga Creek Greenway nearby. The wooded area provides facilities for tent and trailer camping, including waterfront sites.

Henry Horton State Park

Chapel Hill, TN 37034
(615) 364-7724
On U.S. Hwy. 31A. The park is on the old estate of Henry H. Horton, the thirty-sixth governor of Tennessee. It is located on the Duck River, the longest remaining stretch of free-flowing river in the state of Tennessee, which supports the most diverse mussel fauna in the world. The 1,141-acre park provides a seventy-two-room inn, cabins and a restaurant which seats 250 along with meeting room space to accommodate convention and family

groups. The park's eighteen-hole championship golf course, with bent grass greens and a pro shop, is one of the finest in the state. A challenging "Disc Golf Course" is also available. The state park system's only skeet and trap range is located here. Family canoeing is also popular on the scenic Duck River. Camping and swimming are available. Nearby is Nathan Bedford Forrest's boyhood home.

House Mountain
State Natural Area

3903 Idumea Road
Corryton, TN 37721
(615) 933-6851

Off U.S. Hwy. 11W. Five-hundred-acre House Mountain reaches 2,100 feet above sea level and is well worth its steep hike to see the distant Smoky Mountains and the undulating Ridge and Valley country of East Tennessee. Chestnut oak, table mountain pine, and pitch pine crown the sandstone summit. Migrating hawks and songbirds and lush wildflowers are seen in season. House Mountain is located eleven miles from the Knoxville Zoo on 11W North.

Indian Mountain State Park

Jellico, TN 37762
(615) 784-7958

Off I-75 at exit 160. Located in the Cumberland Mountains within the city limits of Jellico, this two-hundred-acre park is popular with campers. The park is unique in that it was developed on reclaimed strip-mine land. Two small lakes provide fishing opportunities. Paddle boats are available for rent, and there is a three-fourths-mile walking trail adjacent to the campground.

Johnsonville State Historic Park

Route 1, Box 37-4
New Johnsonville, TN 37134
(615) 535-2789

Off U.S. Hwy. 70. Named for Military Governor Andrew Johnson, this 550-acre park on the eastern side of Kentucky Lake overlooks the site of the battle of Johnsonville. Cavalry forces under Lt. Gen. Nathan Bedford Forrest sank four Federal gunboats downstream and destroyed a Union Army supply depot at Johnsonville. Four of the original breastworks are beautifully preserved. Interpretive tours are available.

Long Hunter State Park

2910 Hobson Pike
Hermitage, TN 37076
(615) 885-2422

Off I-40 and I-24 on State Route 171. Named after the early explorers of the 1700s, Long Hunter is located along the shore of the U.S. Army Corps of Engineers Percy Priest Reservoir. The 2,315-acre park offers a variety of day-use recreational opportunities and protects a unique cedar glade environment. The Couchville Area is totally barrier-free and has a 110-acre lake with a fishing pier. A visitors center provides exhibits and key information on the park's unique flora and fauna. No individual campsites are available. This park features twenty-eight miles of hiking trails suitable for day hiking and overnight backpacking. The park is barrier free.

Montgomery Bell State Park

P.O. Box 39, Burns, TN 37029
(615) 797-3101

North of I-40 on U.S. 70. The 3,782-acre park is in the rolling hills of the Western Highland Rim, seven miles east of Dickson. Brown iron ore lured Montgomery Bell, the park's namesake, from his native Pennsylvania. Here he established an extensive iron industry in the Dickson County area. Laurel furnace, built in 1810, and the old ore pits of this long-silenced industry are still visible. The park is also the site of the birthplace of the Cumberland Presbyterian Church. Organized in 1810, the church is commemorated by a replica of the Rev. Samuel McAdow's log house and a chapel where summer services welcome all. Worth seeing are the old white oaks, rocky streams, and the Hall Spring that flows at a rate of 1,100 gallons per minute.

Mousetail Landing State Park

Route 3, Box 280 B
Linden, TN 37096
(901) 847-0841

On State Hwy. 50. This 1,249-acre area is located on the east banks of the Tennessee River in the state's picturesque Western Valley. Tradition has it that Mousetail Landing received its name during the Civil War period when one of the area's tanning companies caught fire. The exodus of mice fleeing the burning tannery was so profuse, that the area in proximity of the park became known as Mousetail Landing. The scenic Buffalo River flows nearby, providing opportunity for family canoe float trips.

Nathan Bedford Forrest
State Park

Star Route, Eva, TN 38333
(901) 584-6356

North of I-40 near Camden on State Hwy. 191. On the western side of Kentucky Lake, Pilot Knob is this

2,587-acre park's most prominent point. Named for its use as a landmark by riverboat pilots, it overlooks the site of the Civil War battle of Johnsonville and is the home of the Tennessee River Folklife Museum. The 741-foot Pilot Knob offers a spectacular view of the Western Valley of the Tennessee River. A monument commemorating Nathan Bedford Forrest is adjacent to the visitors center.

Norris Dam State Park

1261 Norris Freeway
Lake City, TN 37769
(615) 426-7461
East of I-75 on U.S. Hwy. 441. This 4,038-acre park is located on Norris Reservoir, begun in 1933 as the first Tennessee Valley Authority project. Miles of trails lead hikers through deeply forested valleys and ridges. A grist mill built in the 1790s and restored by TVA still grinds corn daily during the summer months. Adjacent to the mill is a threshing barn and the W. G. Lenoir Museum, displaying a remarkable collection of pioneer artifacts from the area. A short distance south on U.S. 441, America's first scenic (limited access) parkway, is the Museum of Appalachia.

Old Stone Fort State Archaeological Park

Route 7, Box 7400
Manchester, TN 37355
(615) 723-5073
On U.S. Hwy. 41, one and one-half miles off I-24. The Old Stone Fort is an earth-and-stone enclosure, built as a sacred site by prehistoric Woodland Indians almost two thousand years ago. The picturesque waterfalls

of both forks of the Duck River also attracted nineteenth-century industries, the ruins of which are still visible. A one-and-one-fourth-mile walk with interpretive booklet follows the wall and cliff perimeter. May Prairie is nearby, a prairie remnant containing dozens of rare plants. Interpretive tours are available.

Panther Creek State Park

2010 Panther Creek Road
Morristown, TN 37814
(615) 587-7046
West of I-81 just off U.S. Hwy. 11E. Located on Cherokee Reservoir in the historic Holston River Valley, this 1,440-acre park is six miles west of Morristown. It is named for nearby Panther Creek Springs, a pioneer landmark. A 1,460-foot ridge provides a panoramic view of the East Tennessee Ridge and Valley region. Bird watchers gather at this high vantage point to observe migrating hawks and waterfowl. Camping, swimming, and picnicking are available.

Paris Landing State Park

Route 1, Buchanan, TN 38222
(901) 642-4311
On U.S. Hwy. 79. Located on the western shore of 158,300-acre Kentucky Lake, Paris Landing is named for a steamboat-and-freight landing dating back to the mid-1800s. Today, there is a 100-room inn with an excellent dining room and complete convention and meeting facilities. Fishing, boating, and other water sports are very popular on the lake. Camping, swimming, and a marina are available. The park's eighteen-hole championship golf course has

bent grass greens and a pro shop. Nearby are the Big Sandy Unit of the Tennessee Wildlife Refuge, the 170,000-acre TVA Land Between the Lakes, and the Fort Donelson National Military Park.

Pickwick Landing State Park

P.O. Box 15
Pickwick Dam, TN 38365
(901) 689-3135
On State Hwy. 57 at Pickwick Dam. This 1,392-acre park on the shores of Pickwick Reservoir is a water sportsman's paradise. A full-service marina includes dry boat storage, sailboat, wet, and overnight slips. Three public launching ramps are provided. From the park it is possible to lock through Pickwick Dam for a scenic cruise down the Tennessee River of over 150 miles, passing Shiloh National Military Park, historic Savannah, and the Tennessee National Wildlife Refuge. A seventy-two-room inn and a restaurant provide convention and meeting facilities. An eighteen-hole championship golf course is also available.

Pinson Mounds State Archaeological Park

460 Ozier Road, Pinson, TN 38366
(901) 988-5614
Off U.S. Hwy. 45. This 1,086-acre prehistoric Indian ceremonial center contains the second highest mound in the United States. Archaeological research is conducted on-site and at the museum; park visitors are welcome to view these scientific activities. Self-guided trails enable visitors to learn about the early inhabitants of this expansive site. A boardwalk trail along the Forked Deer River showcases the area's natural beauty.

Port Royal State Historic Park

3300 Old Clarksville Hwy.
Adams, TN 37010
(615) 358-9696
State Route 76. An area rich in history, twenty-six-acre Port Royal is the site of one of Tennessee's earliest communities and trading centers. Today it is a place of quiet beauty featuring a covered bridge spanning the Red River. Interpretive walks and talks are available on request.

Red Clay State Historic Park

1140 Red Clay Road SE
Cleveland, TN 37311
(615) 478-0339
Off of U.S. Hwy. 60 south of Cleveland, on the Georgia border. Banned from meeting in their nearby capital of New Echota, Red Clay was the site of the last Cherokee Councils before the infamous Trail of Tears. An interpretive center and replicas of Cherokee structures of the 1830s depict the life of the Cherokee. Several short trails lead to the Eternal Flame and the enchanting Blue Spring.

Rock Island State Park

Route 2, Box 20
Rock Island, TN 38581
(615) 686-2471
U.S. Hwy. 70S. The scenic beauty of this wooded park is dominated by the Great Falls of the Caney Fork River—an imposing limestone gorge (called a gulf in southern culture). It provides scenic overlooks, waterfalls, and deep pools for fishing, rock-hopping, and exploring. Located at the confluence of the Collins and Caney Fork rivers, this 883-acre

park has a natural sand beach on Center Hill Reservoir. Tours of nearby Big Bone Cave are available upon request. Historic features of the park include a nineteenth-century textile mill and one of Tennessee's early hydroelectric plants.

Sergeant Alvin C. York Historic Park

General Delivery
Pall Mall, TN 38577
(615) 879-4026
On U.S. Hwy. 127. Located in Pall Mall, seven miles north of Jamestown, this park pays tribute to Sgt. Alvin C. York, one of the most decorated soldiers of World War I. The site includes the York home place, gravesite, school, family farm, and the grist mill he operated on the banks of the Wolf River.

Standing Stone State Park

1674 Standing Stone Park Highway
Hilham, TN 38568
(615) 823-6347
Off State Hwy. 52. Named for an eight-foot-tall rock that once served as a boundary line between separate Indian nations, this 1,055-acre park within a large state forest combines outstanding scenery and recreational opportunities. Rental rowboats are available for those wanting to fish the sixty-nine-acre Standing Stone Lake, and fifteen miles of hiking trail meander through the hills and hollows. The park is five miles from Dale Hollow Reservoir, one of Tennessee's most scenic impoundments. Standing Stone is the site of the National Rollyhole Marbles Championship held each September.

Sycamore Shoals State Historic Park

1651 West Elk Avenue
Elizabethton, TN 37643
(615) 543-5808
On U.S. Hwy. 321. A museum and a reconstruction of Fort Watauga, which was excavated about a mile away on the shores of the Watauga River, are open daily. The museum and fort interpret the role this area played in eighteenth-century history as the state of Franklyn in the expansion of America's western boundary. Here, the Overmountain Men mustered in September 1780 before their march to fight the battle of King's Mountain. Tours of the nearby eighteenth-century Carter Mansion are also available by appointment. Nearby is the Covered Bridge Park along the Doe River.

T. O. Fuller State Park

1500 Mitchell Road West
Memphis, TN 38109
(901) 543-7581
West of U.S. Hwy. 61, near Interstates 40 and 50. Named after prominent Memphis clergyman and educator Dr. Thomas Oscar Fuller, this 384-acre park is eleven miles southwest of downtown Memphis. The park is adjacent to historic Chucalissa Indian Village, operated by Memphis State University. Chucalissa includes a Choctaw village reconstruction, preserved archaeological excavations, and a modern museum. Park facilities include an eighteen-hole golf course, a swimming pool, picnicking areas, and campsites.

Tims Ford State Park

570 Tims Ford Drive
Winchester, TN 37398
(615) 967-4457
Off State Hwy. 50. Located on 10,700-acre Tims Ford Reservoir this 413-acre park sits in the shadows of the Cumberland Plateau in South Central Tennessee. Although the park is oriented toward fishing and water recreation, it offers five miles of paved bike trails with bike rentals, a hiking trail, cabins, camping, swimming, and a boat dock. The historic towns of Lynchburg, Cowan, and Sewanee are nearby.

Warriors' Path State Park

P.O. Box 5026
Kingsport, TN 37663
(615) 239-8531
From I-81 take exit 59 to State Route 36. Located on the shores of Fort Patrick Henry Reservoir, this 950-acre park was named for its proximity to ancient war and trading paths used by the Cherokee. While the park is water-activity oriented, nine miles of hiking trail meander through woodlands and up the Holston Bluffs to the scenic Devil's Backbone. Recreational amenities include an eighteen-hole golf course, miniature golf course and driving range, swimming pool and water slide, a "disc golf course," a marina, campground, and boat-launch facilities. Nearby is Bays Mountain Nature Center.

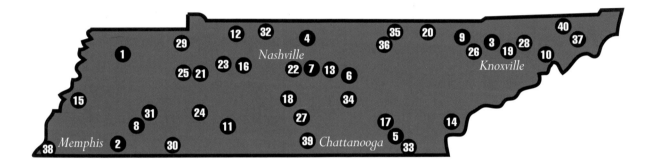

1 Big Cypress Tree State Natural Area	**14** Fort Loudoun State Historic Park	**26** Norris Dam State Park
2 Big Hill Pond State Park	**15** Fort Pillow State Historic Park	**27** Old Stone Fort State Archaeological Park
3 Big Ridge State Park	**16** Harpeth Scenic River and Narrows Historic Area	**28** Panther Creek State Park
4 Bledsoe Creek State Park	**17** Harrison Bay State Park	**29** Paris Landing State Park
5 Booker T. Washington State Park	**18** Henry Horton State Park	**30** Pickwick Landing State Park
6 Burgess Falls State Natural Area	**19** House Mountain State Natural Area	**31** Pinson Mounds State Archaeological Park
7 Cedars of Lebanon State Park	**20** Indian Mountain State Park	**32** Port Royal State Historic Park
8 Chickasaw State Park	**21** Johnsonville State Historic Park	**33** Red Clay State Historic Park
9 Cove Lake State Park	**22** Long Hunter State Park	**34** Rock Island State Park
10 Davy Crockett Birthplace State Park	**23** Montgomery Bell State Park	**35** Sergeant Alvin C. York Historic Park
11 David Crockett State Park	**24** Mousetail Landing State Park	**36** Standing Stone State Park
12 Dunbar Cave State Natural Area	**25** Nathan Bedford Forrest State Park	**39** Tims Ford State Park
13 Edgar Evins State Park		**40** Warriors' Path State Park